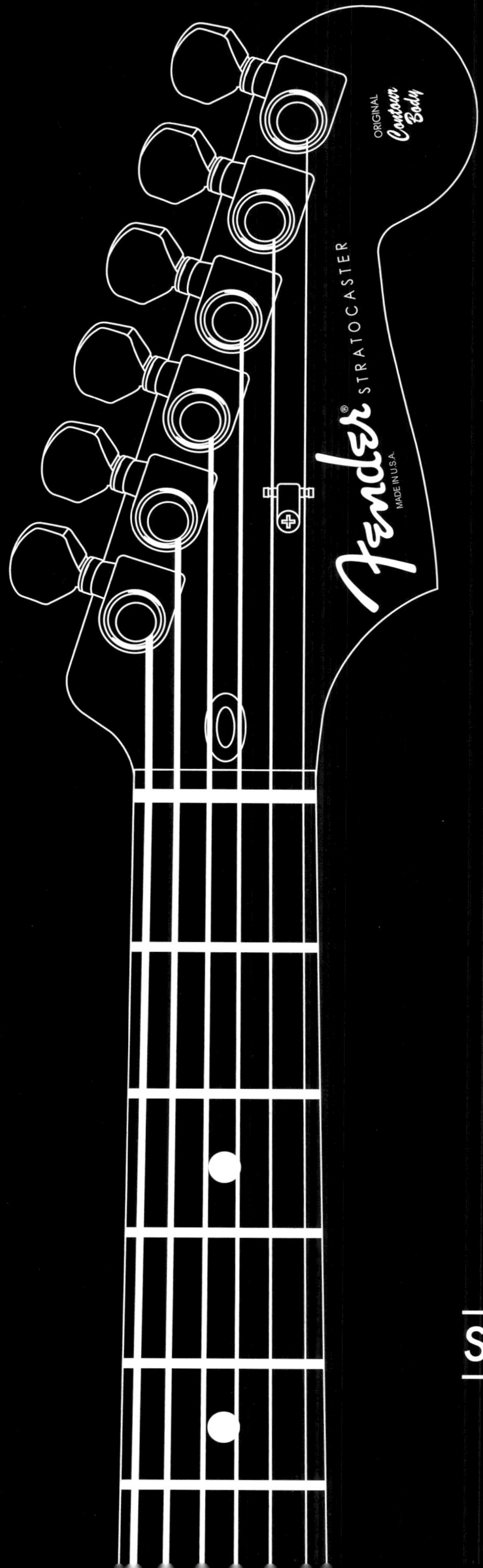

Fender®

70th Anniversary

STRATOCASTER®

1954 • 2024

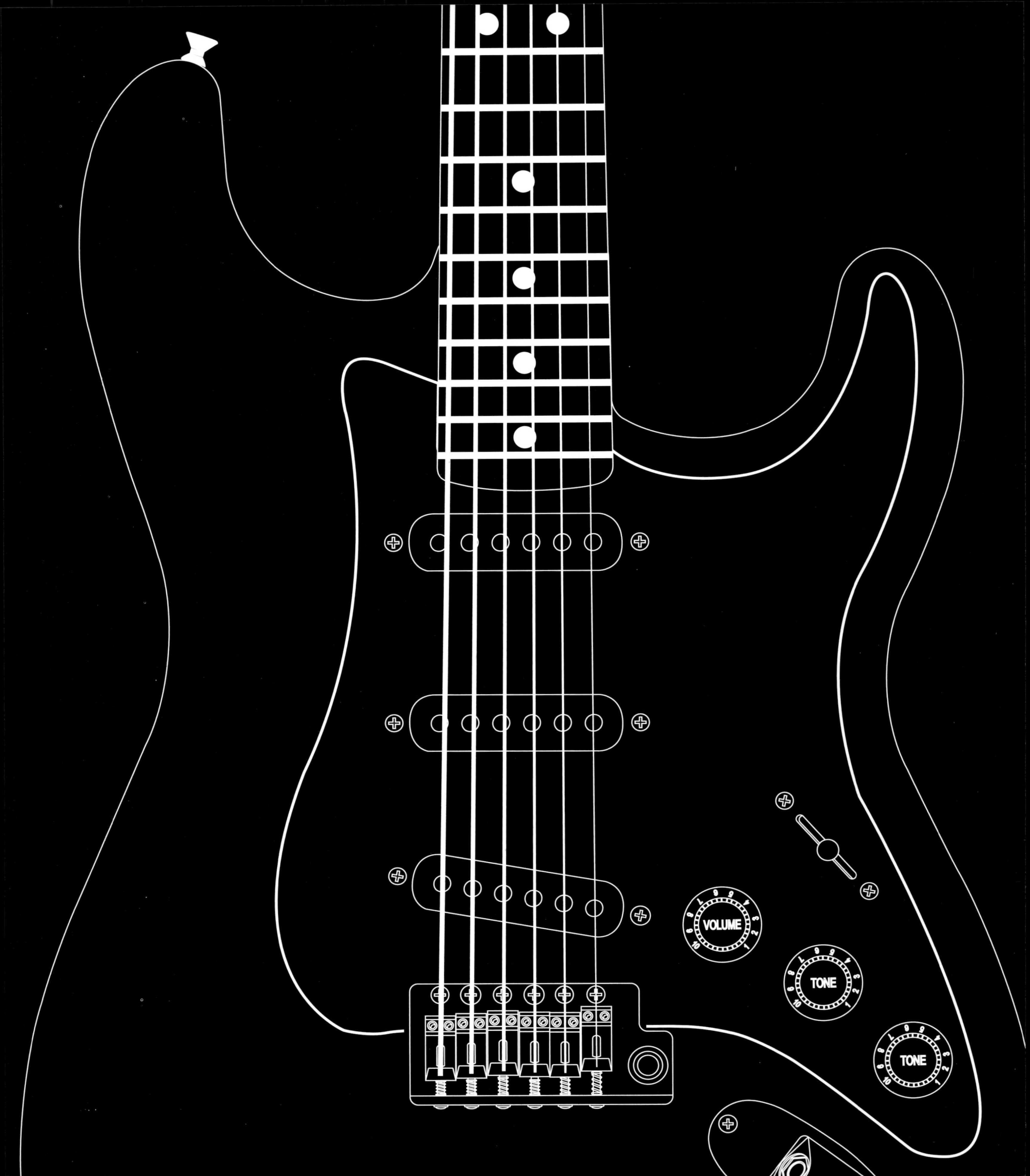
VOLUME
TONE
TONE

Fender®

STRATOCASTER 70 YEARS

DAVE HUNTER

Foreword by Nile Rodgers

Contents

Foreword by Nile Rodgers

It's 1973 and I was asleep at a run-down '50s-era motel in South Florida. Suddenly I was awakened by loud music emanating from a passing car. My head hit the open drawer above me that housed my chocolate cookies. The stinky bed sagged and my butt hit the floor. This trio of mishaps ended my restless slumber. I left the motel to get an early breakfast and plan the rest of my day. The only diner within walking distance was equally abysmal. Everything was in tragic alignment. It felt like the beginning of the worst day of my life.

The night before, my Big Apple Band, which backed an R&B vocal group called New York City, had just played a Miami hotspot called The Castaways. New York City had a hit single called "I'm Doin' Fine Now," so we were headlining.

Our opening act had a guitar player whose technical facilities were basic, but his guitar sound smoked mine. To make matters worse, he was playing through my amp. His guitar was a Fender Stratocaster and my guitar was a Barney Kessel, as back in those days I was more of a jazz and classical session player.

My partner was one of the greatest musicians of all time: a bassist named Bernard Edwards. He played a Fender Jazz Bass and would scream these words at me daily, "Get a Strat, motherf***er!" What finally convinced me to get a Strat was not his constant berating, but the great sound of an average guitar player in an opening band.

I was playing smash hit songs on my jazz box, but I knew our opening act's guitar sound was better for my gig. No longer would I have to put up with Bernard's screaming, because now I was going to buy a Stratocaster.

As I started my quest it hit me that I knew nothing about the Stratocaster on a player's level, but I had a stable pop gig and wanted to do my best to keep it. A Stratocaster seemed to be the right tool for the right job.

I walked along Dixie Highway, the main drag for Miami pawnshops back then. The shops were flooded with all manner of guitars. So many were hung on the walls that it almost looked like a guitar crucifixion site. I was about to become one Stratocaster's savior.

Since I knew nothing about the performance of the Stratocaster, I just went for the lowest-priced one. My heart broke as I handed my Barney Kessel over the counter to complete the trade. However, as soon as I pulled that Strat down from the dusty wall, sadness was instantly replaced with joy—and to my utter surprise, they gave me an additional three hundred bucks. I guess that was the difference in the pawnshop book value.

I ecstatically returned to my motel room and started to practice "chucking," a technique where you continuously play 16th notes with the right hand while judiciously striking or muting notes with the left.

I practiced every minute I could. I shared a room with our band's drummer. When he was around, I'd go into the bathroom's shower so as not to disturb him. After a few weeks I emerged from the bathroom a funky new player. I could cleanly chuck anywhere on the neck and my Fender Stratocaster responded perfectly. Its tone was so consistent that I barely touched the "speed knobs" that I had put on to play crying sounds.

I don't know what it is that makes my Strat so special. It's thinner and lighter than any I've ever seen. I heard folklore from Fender aficionados saying that Leo Fender was the cheapest man that ever lived and that in 1959 he made a bad deal on a bulk buy of ash that turned out to be overpriced. To compensate, he squeezed a few extra bodies out of it, making them more slender than usual. Some people even mistake it for a Mary Kaye. I just know it fits me like a glove and back in that pawnshop in Miami fifty years ago the universe delivered me a Strat that changed my life!

I fell in love and I fell in love hard. It didn't take long to realize why those who came before and after me, like Jimi Hendrix, Jeff Beck, Ritchie Blackmore, Eric Clapton, Kurt Cobain, The Edge, John Frusciante, Rory Gallagher, David Gilmour, Buddy Guy, George Harrison, Eddie Hazel, Buddy Holly, Ernie Isley, Mark Knopfler, John Mayer, Richie Sambora, Ike Turner, Eddie Van Halen, Stevie Ray Vaughan, Cory Wong, Ronnie Wood, and thousands of others—many of whom I went on to produce—felt the same way. This was an instrument that changed and is still changing the world! Put a Strat in the hands of the right person and the possibilities are endless!

Fifty years have passed since I pulled that cheap guitar off that wall and it has never let me down. People know it today as "The Hitmaker" because it's played on everything from thousands of live gigs to films, video games, and theatrical productions, and is responsible for over 500 million albums sold on the biggest recordings from CHIC, Sister Sledge, Diana Ross, David Bowie, Madonna, Duran Duran, Daft Punk, Beyoncé, and countless others. From "Le Freak" to "Let's Dance," "Get Lucky," and "Cuff It," people the world over know the sound of my Strat! After five decades, I still carry it slung over my shoulder in a gig bag. People freak out because they know it's priceless, but to me it makes sense. I originally bought it to keep a gig, and in return it keeps me gigging.

With deepest gratitude,
Nile Rodgers

Nile Rodgers with the Custom Shop rendition of his "Hitmaker" Stratocaster.

Chapter

1

A BRIDGE TO THE FUTURE

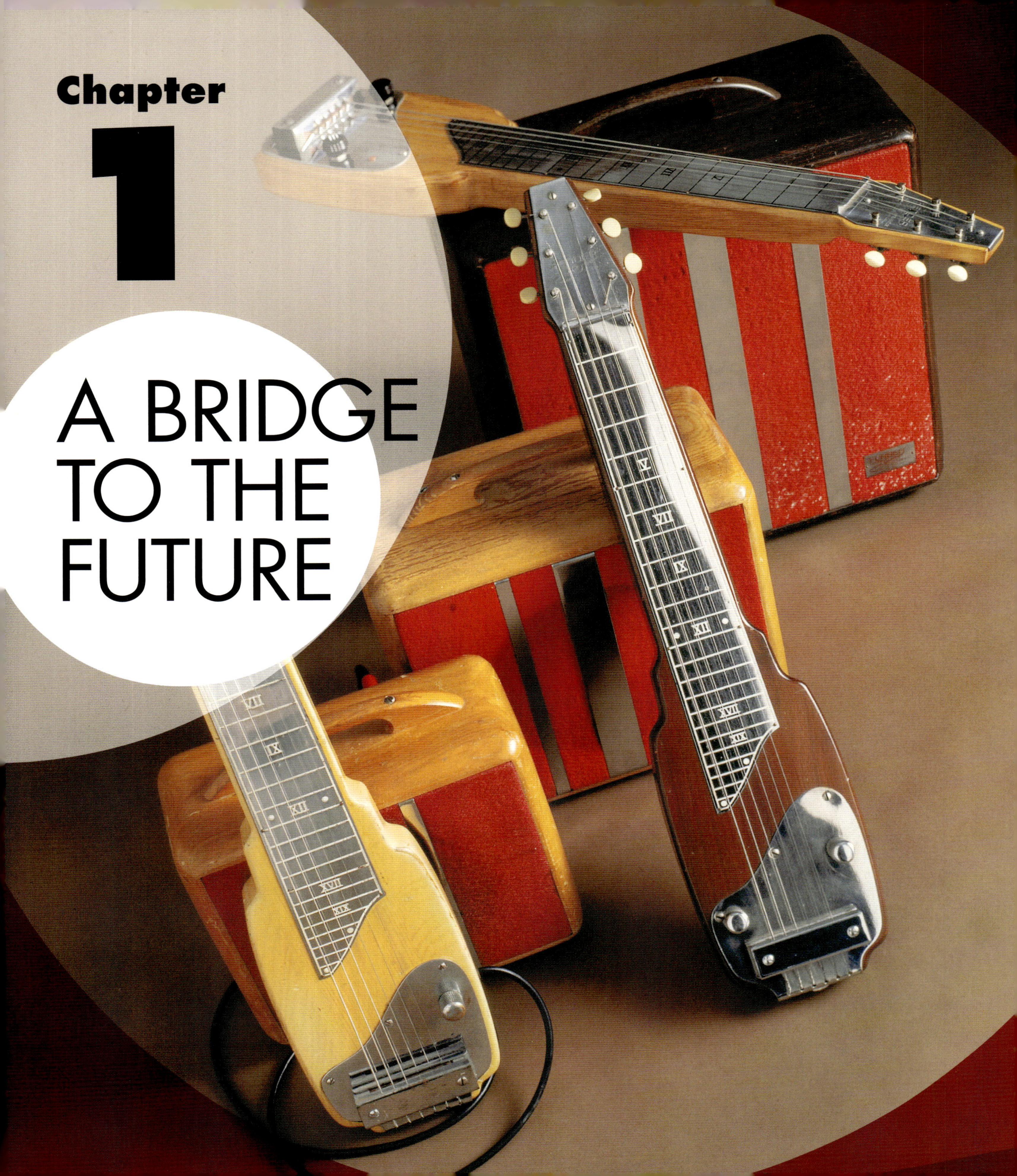

A Groundbreaking Guitar Company Is Born

Fender's lap-steel and wood-cabinet amplifier lineup of 1946–1947.

Sublimely stylish, sleekly space-aged, and graced with unprecedented playability and sonic versatility, the Fender Stratocaster was clearly well ahead of its time upon its public unveiling in 1954, and arguably its capabilities wouldn't be fully appreciated for a decade or more to come. It's amazing to think, then, that the seeds of this groundbreaking design were sown so many years before that, in entirely different eras of art and industry.

The story of the most innovative and imitated electric guitar of all time perhaps begins a decade and a half before its inception, when its creator took the gamble of turning his hobby into his vocation and started down the road that would lead surprisingly quickly to one of the most revolutionary music-making machines ever conceived. Or we could say it began another three decades before that, when the household name on the headstock was brought into this world and began the journey that would form and inform his curiosity and creativity.

The gulf between 1938 and 1954 brought unprecedented changes to both the United States and the world. The leap between these years spans the simplicity and relative innocence of the late-Depression, prewar year in which Leo Fender started his radio electronics business, and the postwar age in which so much of his work came to fruition, right alongside the burgeoning Cold War and a few strides short of the Space Race. In a very real sense, this era formed a bridge between a much earlier and even ancient-seeming America and one on the cusp of modernity, just beginning to toddle toward the world we live in today.

If we can sum up the forward-thrusting posture of 1954 in the form of any musical instrument, the lithe, futuristic curves of the Stratocaster must surely be it. This is a guitar packed with potential, and its increasing success at aiding and abetting year upon year and decade upon decade of cutting-edge music only confirms how revolutionary it was at its birth. But to get to this point, we need to look briefly at where Leo started and give some thought to the considerable achievements that led up to what has arguably been his greatest contribution to the sound of popular music and how it was made.

Leo's Early Years

Convert in your mind's eye the seemingly endless sprawl of the greater Los Angeles metropolitan area of today to a gently rolling oasis of orange groves and small agricultural holdings, laced with the occasional main street and business district. Now you're looking at Fullerton, California, where Clarence Leonidas Fender was born on August 10, 1909. His parents, Clarence and Harriet, were orange growers, and young Leo spent his youth as a farm boy, albeit one who was afforded the opportunity of an education primed to take him off the farm, while his diverse interests helped him dream of things even further afield.

From an early age, Leo showed an interest in pursuits that, while pretty ordinary or even old-fashioned from our twenty-first-century perspective, would have been very forward-looking and cutting-edge for his time. He was fascinated with electronics, radios, and amplification in particular, and he showed an interest in popular music styles. It is widely written that Leo Fender never learned to play the guitar, but to imply that he wasn't musical or didn't have "an ear" would be a falsehood. He learned to play the piano somewhat and was even more proficient on the saxophone, which he played in the school orchestra.

He also built a guitar from scratch while still in his mid-teens, pursuing a drive to tinker in general. More importantly, perhaps, while only ever an amateur musician himself, he showed a great appreciation for the skills of professional players and an innate understanding of what they needed from their instruments, as well as a willingness to listen to their assessments of qualities that he couldn't initially perceive himself.

It's notable that Leo Fender came into music electronics from the amplification side of the equation, a perspective that likely informed his approach to much of his instrument-design efforts in the future.

ABOVE: *A young and sharply dressed Leo leans on the running board of the family car.* RIGHT: *Leo as a pupil in front of Fullerton Union High School.* OPPOSITE: *In his youth, Leo played the saxophone, trumpet, and piano.*

He attended local public schools throughout his youth, and although he had no formal training in electronics, he built radios and other devices in his teens while showing an aptitude for all things mechanical. An uncle, John West, ran an auto shop in Santa Maria, California, and aided his nephew's hobby one Christmas by sending him a box loaded with salvaged electronic components. To the ardent hobbyist, it was a bottomless box of possibilities.

Of a visit to his uncle's shop, Leo recalled much later, "He had built some radio equipment and had a large wooden trumpet speaker in front of his shop, pointed downtown to [amplify] radio programs. This acquainted me with radio and led to my building amplifiers for musicians."[1]

Upon graduating from Fullerton Union High School in 1928, Leo studied accounting at Fullerton Junior College, eventually taking a two-year diploma, moving on to a series of bookkeeping jobs, and marrying his first wife, Esther, in 1934. All the while, though, his electronics hobby persisted, and soon Leo was making a name for himself as a builder and repairman of just about anything tube-amplified. Leo's tinkering led local bands to ask him to build PA systems in his spare time, and soon the hobby blossomed into a thriving sideline, building, renting out, and maintaining PAs used at musical and sporting events around the Orange County area. The Great Depression, however, was a tough time for a guy trained to count money; when the tire company he was working for in San Luis Obispo cut its entire accounting department in 1938, Leo and Esther made the leap. They took a loan of $600, returned to his home turf of Fullerton, and opened his first shop: Fender's Radio Service.

Radios and More

Although he certainly repaired the radios that gave his business its name, Leo Fender did much more than that in his little storefront in Fullerton. Soon the place was regarded as a full-service business addressing the needs of local music fans and musicians, becoming a noted casual hang for the latter. Fender's Radio Service sold radios, records, and record players, but Leo also put a lot of time into repairing instruments and amplifiers that were brought in by local musicians, who were soon asking him to build them new and better amps and PA systems.

By all accounts, Leo loved the work. He had a propensity to listen to the needs of musicians and a knack for discerning the flaws in existing designs—two traits that would greatly inform his approaches to the design and construction of electric instruments and amplifiers, helping distinguish Fender creations amid a crowded marketplace.

"Originally my work was design, modification, repair, and custom building," Leo said in 1971. "This gave me a wide acquaintance with competitive products and users' needs. Since my work encompassed more than musical equipment, I knew of benefits I could apply to the musicians' gear. I guess you would say the objectives were durability, performance, and tone."[2]

118 RADIO

FENDER'S RADIO SERVICE

RADIO SALES, SERVICE & RENTALS

- ELECTRICAL APPLIANCES
- PHONOGRAPH RECORDS
- MUSICAL INSTRUMENTS & REPAIRS
- PUBLIC ADDRESS SYSTEMS
- SHEET MUSIC

SPECIALIZING IN "EVERY BRANCH OF SOUND"

107 SO. SPADRA — FULLERTON — TELEPHONE 6

TOP: *A busy South Harbor Boulevard in Fullerton, California, around the time the Fender company was getting established.* OPPOSITE TOP: *Pressing records was just one "branch of sound" offered by Fender's Radio Service.* OPPOSITE BOTTOM: *The site of Fender's Radio Service at 107 South Spadra as it appears today.*

FENDER'S
RADIO SERVICE
Radios • Records • Phonographs
107 S. SPADRA, FULLERTON
Phone 6
FOR A COLORFUL REPRODUCTION
FENDER'S
RADIO SERVICE
112 SO. SPADRA, FULLERTON CALIF.
Phone 1257
Motorola
Packard Bell
Radios-Recorders
ARTIST:
TITLE:
DATE:
RAINBO RECORD CO. LOS ANGELES

ELLINGSON
Est. 1946
107
CITY OF FULLERTON
LOCAL LANDMARK
NO. 83
FULLERTON NEWS TRIBUNE
FENDER'S RADIO SERVICE
BUILT CIRCA 1911
CITY OF FULLERTON
CALIFORNIA
Fullerton
Heritage
PLAQUE PLACED BY FULLERTON HERITAGE 2011

Having lost one eye in a childhood accident, Leo was sidelined from the United States' entry into World War II, but the war effort introduced challenges to his efforts, as it did to virtually all private manufacturing in the country. Even deep into the enforced austerity of the age, however, Leo managed to advance his notion of what the business should be, gradually moving by natural inclination away from the original model of the retail store toward one based in product development and manufacturing.

"I liked developing new items that people needed. Working with tools and equipment was more to my liking than retail sales,"[3] he said in an interview in *Guitar Player* magazine in 1971, and it was clear that even before the war was over, Leo had locked on to a new direction for the business. Putting more and more of his time into building PA systems and musical-instrument amplifiers for sale and rent, he was soon dabbling in designing the magnetic pickups that these instruments required to be amplified in the first place.

In the early 1940s, Leo teamed up with musician and inventor Clayton Orr "Doc" Kauffman, and the pair developed a pickup design in 1943 (which was granted a patent in 1948), as well as a precision 45-rpm record changer, whose design and manufacturing rights they sold for $5,000. With what then would have seemed a hefty chunk of seed money in hand, and having moved to larger premises at 107 South Harbor Boulevard in Fullerton (formerly South Spadra) in 1944, Kauffman and Fender formed the K&F Manufacturing Company in 1945. During its brief run, K&F produced three different tube amplifiers and six models of Hawaiian lap-steel guitars to be played through them before the partnership's demise early the next year.

THIS PAGE: *Leo presses his mobile PA into service at a public event in Fullerton in the 1940s.* OPPOSITE: *A K&F lap-steel guitar and amplifier set, circa 1945. K&F produced three models of tube amps and six models of lap-steel guitars before the partnership's early demise in 1946.*

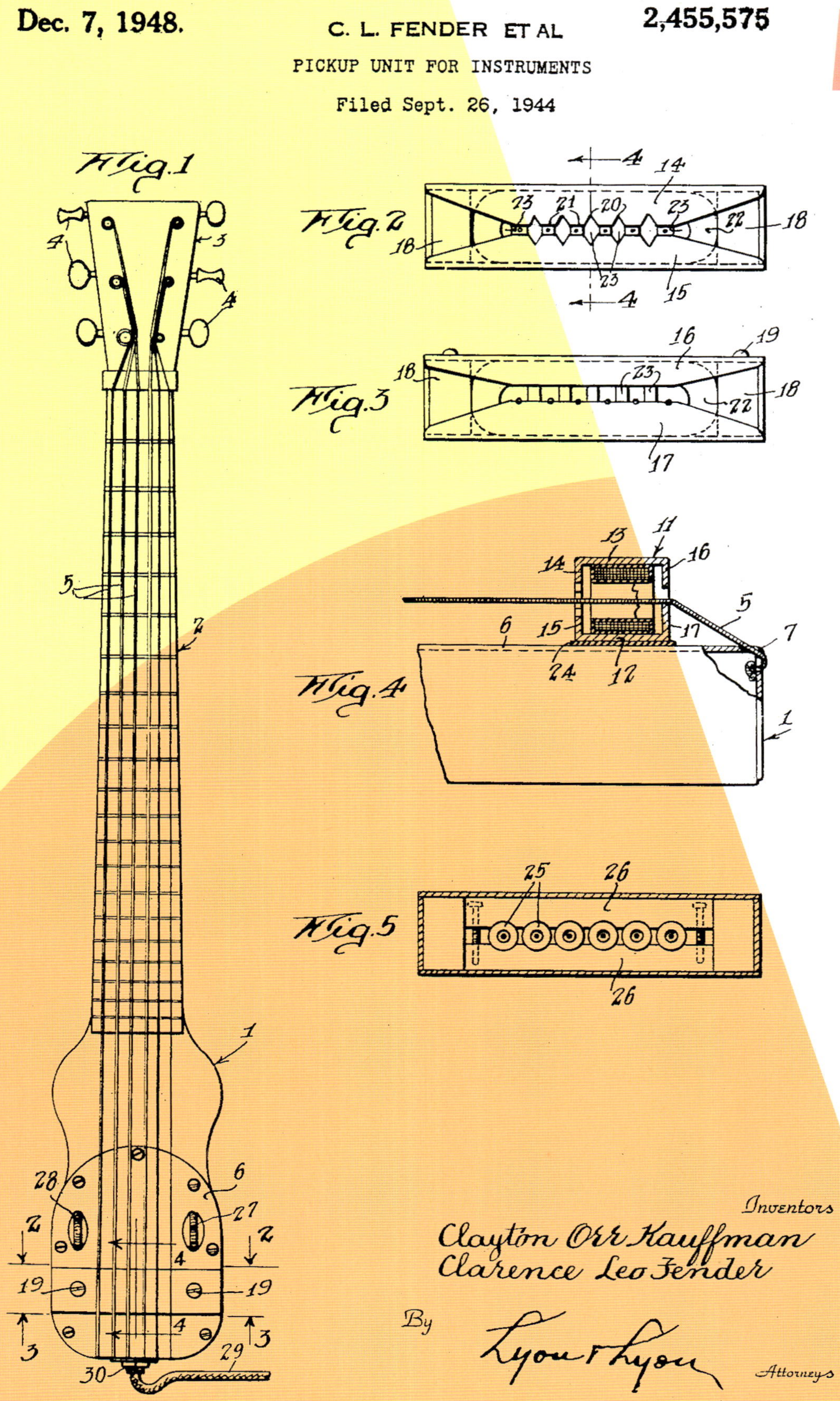

Fender Front and Center

Kauffman quickly grew wary of the risks associated with owning a business, and in February 1946, he traded his interest in K&F to Leo Fender in exchange for a punch press. Leo established the Fender Electric Instrument Company shortly thereafter, and he and the four other employees ported over from K&F continued manufacturing lap-steel guitars and amplifiers that appeared to improve rapidly in quality as Fender devoted his attention more fully to the endeavor.

With the shift to the new company, Fender also began to partner with a new distributor, Radio & Television Equipment Company (Radio-Tel) in Santa Ana. Leo had been purchasing electronic components from Radio-Tel for several years and had developed a good working relationship with its general manager, Don Randall, who would play an enormous role in Fender's growth and success through the next two decades. Meanwhile, Randall convinced Radio-Tel's owner, F. C. Hall, that the products made by Fender Electric Instrument Company were worth picking up, and the fledgling maker soon found a wider reach for its wares.

If Fender amplifiers arguably proved Leo's greatest early success, his formative years of building lap-steel guitars and learning from the musicians who played them were crucial in helping distinguish Fender's eventual electric Spanish guitars from anything else already on the scene. Leo's goals of durability, ease of maintenance, and ease of manufacture would be carried over from the amp line to the guitars, but the sonic goals of "performance and tone" would be more directly derived from the input of musicians who played primarily "hillbilly" and western swing. They wanted instruments that were bright, firm, punchy, and feedback-resistant, and Fender knew how to deliver, even before the Esquire and Broadcaster hit the street.

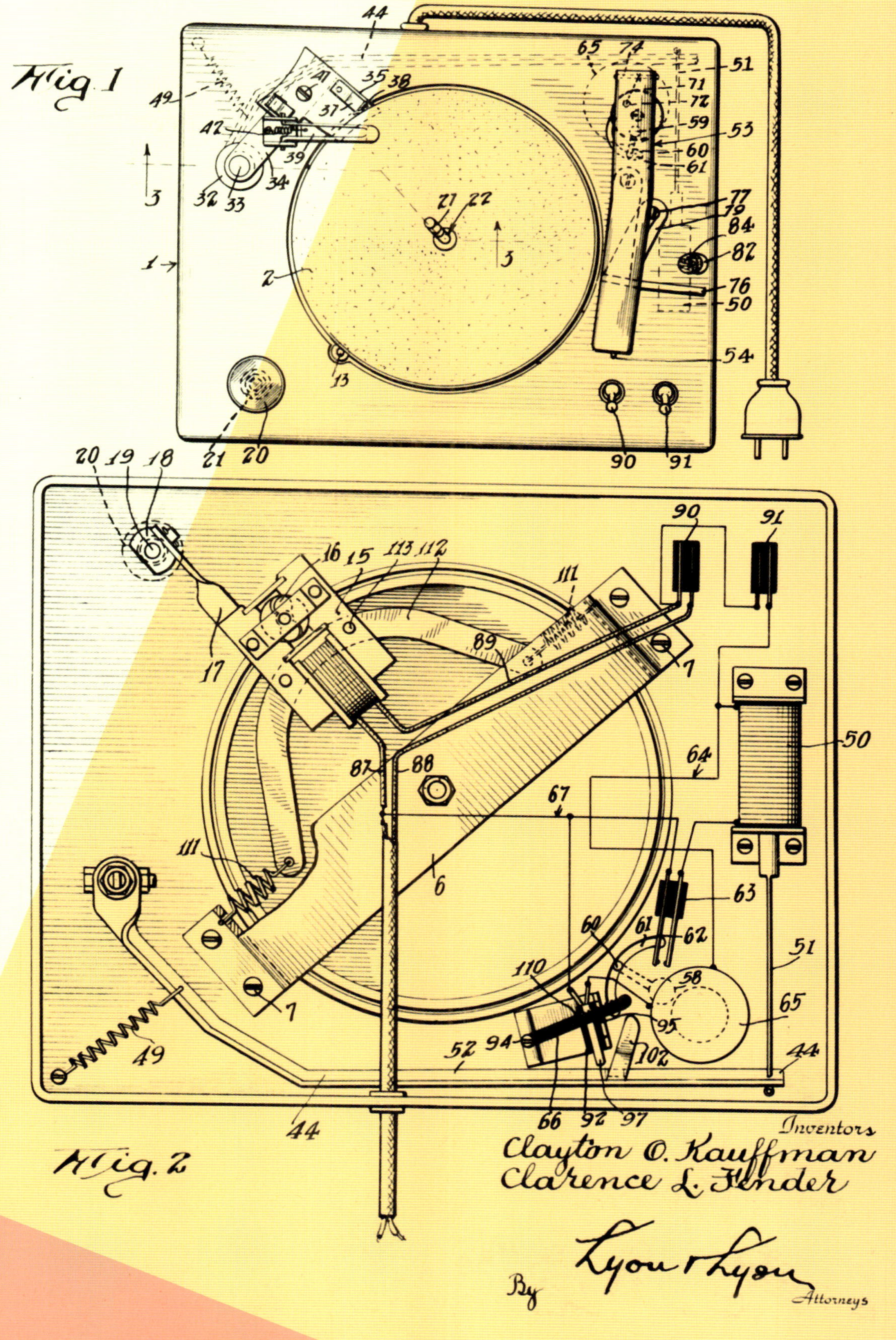

BOTH: *Although their business partnership was short lived, Fender and Kauffman's work together resulted in several patents.*

It's worth noting at this early stage in the game that Fender guitars were not designed to sound like amplified versions of traditional guitars but rather to be an evolution of the existing Hawaiian lap-steel guitars (which displayed the above-mentioned characteristics in abundance) that could be played fretted in the "upright" Spanish style, in standard tuning. Early Fender lap-steel guitars used the "strings-through" pickups (nicknamed "boxcar" pickups) that Leo and Doc had developed for K&F's electric-Hawaiian guitars. These were bright, clear-sounding pickups, although not quite the tone that Fender guitars have been best known for since the early 1950s. In 1948, however, Fender introduced the entry-level Champion amp and lap-steel set (later shortened to Champ), which ushered in a new style of pickup that would set the standard for most Fender pickups to come.

It was made from pressed-fiber top and bottom plates through which six holes were drilled to hold six sections of Alnico rod magnet, around which was wound thousands of turns of wire to form a coil. This is how all noteworthy Fender pickups in the future would be made, with some slight variations in form, including those for the Telecaster, Stratocaster, Jazzmaster, and others.

OPPOSITE: *The pickup on the Champ lap-steel guitar laid the foundation for what was to come.* **RIGHT:** *Irene Vasquez (left) and a colleague laminate lap steel guitars in volatile acetate at the Fender factory.*

With this development, even before the invention of his groundbreaking solid-body guitar, Leo was establishing a bright, cutting yet muscular and twangy tone that would forever help define Fender's sonic signature.

From the earliest days of the amplified guitar, so much of the instrument's evolution was about cutting through the muddy mix of a live band on stage. Brightness and clarity were paramount to that effort and remain beloved hallmarks of Fender guitars today. The early success in achieving this—and firmly establishing "that sound" in an electric-Hawaiian guitar, even before going to market with an electric-Spanish guitar—was a big part of Fender's eventual broader success.

"I think that perhaps I was the first person to use separate magnets, one for each string," he told *Guitar Player* magazine in May 1978. "That way, I found that the notes didn't seem to run together—you could get more of an individual performance off of each string."[4] In addition to the individual magnets, the narrow coil and tight magnetic field also contributed to a bright tone, another boon to the guitarist's effort to "cut through the band."

At the time, more traditional makers such as Gibson, Epiphone, Gretsch, and a few others already had the template for the electric guitar in hand in the form of their existing archtop acoustic guitars and approached musicians' ever-increasing needs for volume primarily from the perspective of amplification. Leo Fender, on the other hand, went at it tone-first, abandoning all preconceptions of the existing form of "the Spanish guitar" and designing his guitar from the ground up. He already knew the sound and how to get it—he just needed a playable and visually acceptable instrument to bolt the pickups to.

Struggling toward the Electric-Spanish Guitar

Fender expanded its manufacturing facilities in the summer of 1947 by constructing a pair of simple metal sheds on Santa Fe Avenue in Fullerton, near the corner of Pomona Avenue. Despite some promising uptake of the amps and electric-Hawaiian guitars, however, the young company often struggled to survive in its early years, and Leo himself was still pursuing several side hustles to make ends meet.

One long-time Fender team member, a former car salesman named Dale Hyatt, joined the company in 1946 and evolved from being a foreman of sorts to overseeing the remaining Fender Radio Shop to playing a major role in sales. George Fullerton—an electronics enthusiast and part-time musician from Arkansas (no connection to the California town where Fender was based)—came to work for Leo early in 1948 with his brothers Bob and Fred. In an interview with author Tony Bacon in the early 1990s, Fullerton talked of Leo's various entrepreneurial sidelines of the mid-1940s:

When I really got acquainted with Leo, there used to be a park in Fullerton on the west side of town called Amerige Park. They would have community happenings. They always had some kind of celebration on the 4th of July, and—I believe it was '47—Leo used to supply the amplifier and sound system for these programs.

Leo had a panel truck, flat-top and long-bodied, and he'd mount speakers on top of it, play music. When they had community happenings he would have somebody drive this van up and down the street advertising the event. There were other occasions that he used these speakers, one was the Sunrise Service on Easter Sunday that used to take place on top of Hillcrest Park.[5]

Even while struggling to survive as a business in the late 1940s, Fender was looking more and more like a real company—all the more so in hindsight, given the major breakthrough that was just around the corner. A photograph taken in 1949 shows most of the company's employees gathered outside one of the sheet-metal buildings that comprised the Fender factory, including Bob Fullerton, Fred Fullerton, George Fullerton, Don Kroener, Lyle Burke, Louis Lugar, Cecil Shawbell, Lawrence Norberg, Lupe Lopez, Lydia Sanchez, Vangie Ortega, and another unidentified man, with others—Irene Vasquez included—believed to have been on the staff but absent from the frame.[6] Also absent are Dale Hyatt, who was still running Fender's Radio Service until its closure in 1951, and Leo himself, a camera buff who may have been on the other side of the lens taking the photo.

ABOVE: *Constructed in 1947, two corrugated metal sheds near the corner of Santa Fe and Pomona Avenues comprised Fender's manufacturing facility. Note the foundation being laid for another building.* OPPOSITE: *Electronics whiz and part-time musician George Fullerton, seen here with his young family, went to work for Leo in 1948.*

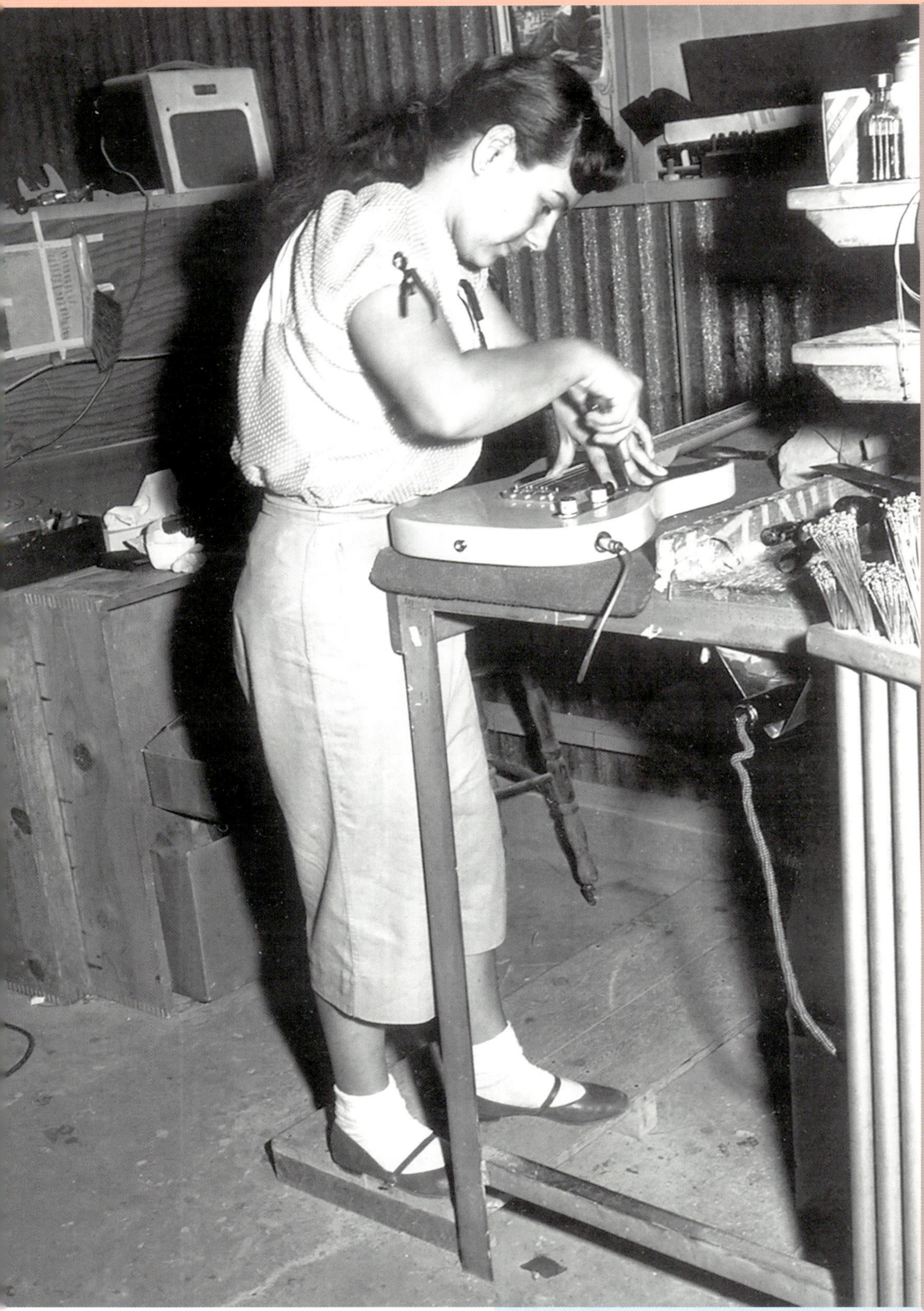

Supplying roadworthy, good-sounding gear to the lap-steel players seemed to be proving a reasonable enough business model for Fender, but plenty of electric-Spanish guitarists strumming other makes of instruments were enjoying the superior performance achieved by plugging these into Fender amplifiers too. Ever observant of local musicians' needs, the gap in the market for a similarly functional, workmanlike electric-Spanish model didn't escape Leo's notice, and toward the end of the 1940s, he and the team got to work on just such a thing. Several prototypes developed through mid-1949 led to production models in early 1950 that were initially called the Esquire (in both single- and two-pickup versions, according to some accounts), a name that stuck with the single-pickup guitars later that year, while the two-pickup model was dubbed the Broadcaster—known from mid-1951 onward as the Telecaster.

Early hiccups like the lack of a truss rod, not to mention some derision from others in the industry, led to improvements on one hand and the will to prove the formula on the other. Clearly, Fender would have the last laugh: whether they play the model themselves or not, few guitarists today fail to acknowledge the Telecaster as a timeless classic, an iconic piece of midcentury-modern guitar design so elegant in its simplicity that it's hard to conceive of it causing any offense. At the time of its release, though, the Telecaster was far from traditional, but that was exactly the point: for players in search of a much-needed new tool to achieve clear, bright, cutting tones in a sonically demanding new form music, it fit the bill exactly.

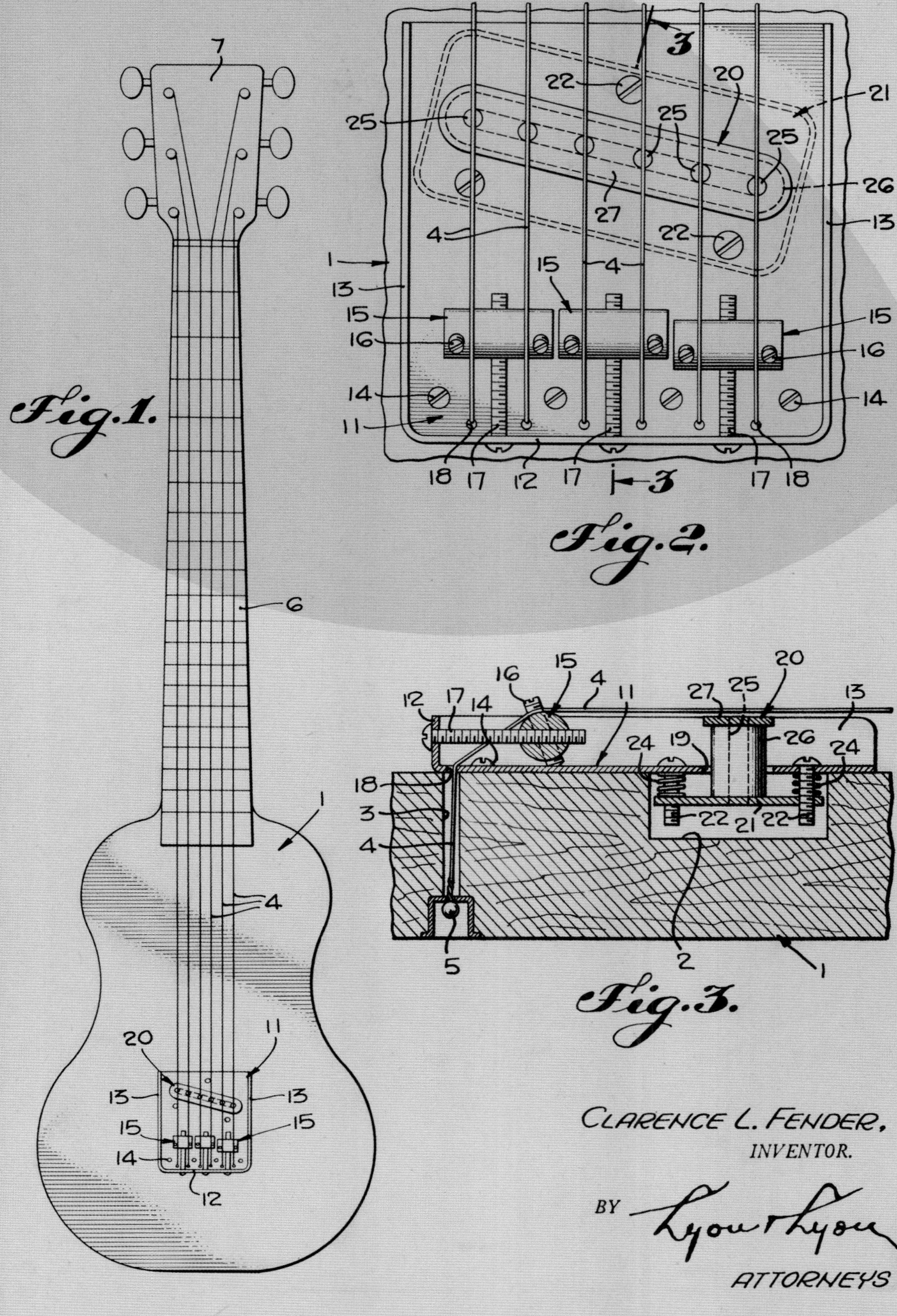

RIGHT: *Leo's patent for the Broadcaster/Telecaster bridge. Early designs hadn't yet adopted the distinctively elegant six-in-line headstock.* **OPPOSITE:** *Final assembly of a Broadcaster, with the corrugated metal walls of Fender's facility in evidence in the background.*

In 1984, Leo Fender told *Guitar Player* magazine of taking a guitar, early in the new solidbody's existence, to the Riverside Rancho Dance Hall in Riverside, California, for up-and-coming country virtuoso Jimmy Bryant to check out. Bryant took it up on stage with Little Jimmy Dickens and his band and started playing, and, as Leo told it, "Pretty soon the band stopped, everybody on the dance floor stopped, and they all gathered around Jimmy when he played."[7]

Guitar players today are likely to think of the solidbody electric as something that's always been with us, but this window into one of the new creation's first public appearances in 1950 hints at just how revolutionary it must have appeared—and sounded. The simple fact was, plank or not, this thing boasted qualities that the hollowbody archtop electrics by Gibson, Gretsch, Epiphone, and so many others just couldn't claim, and it established that essence known as "the Fender sound," defined by a sonic personality that Leo sought to repeat in all his guitars.

ABOVE: *The 1950 Fender catalog.* **LEFT:** *Doc Kauffman returns to Fender in 1950 to check out the new Broadcaster.*

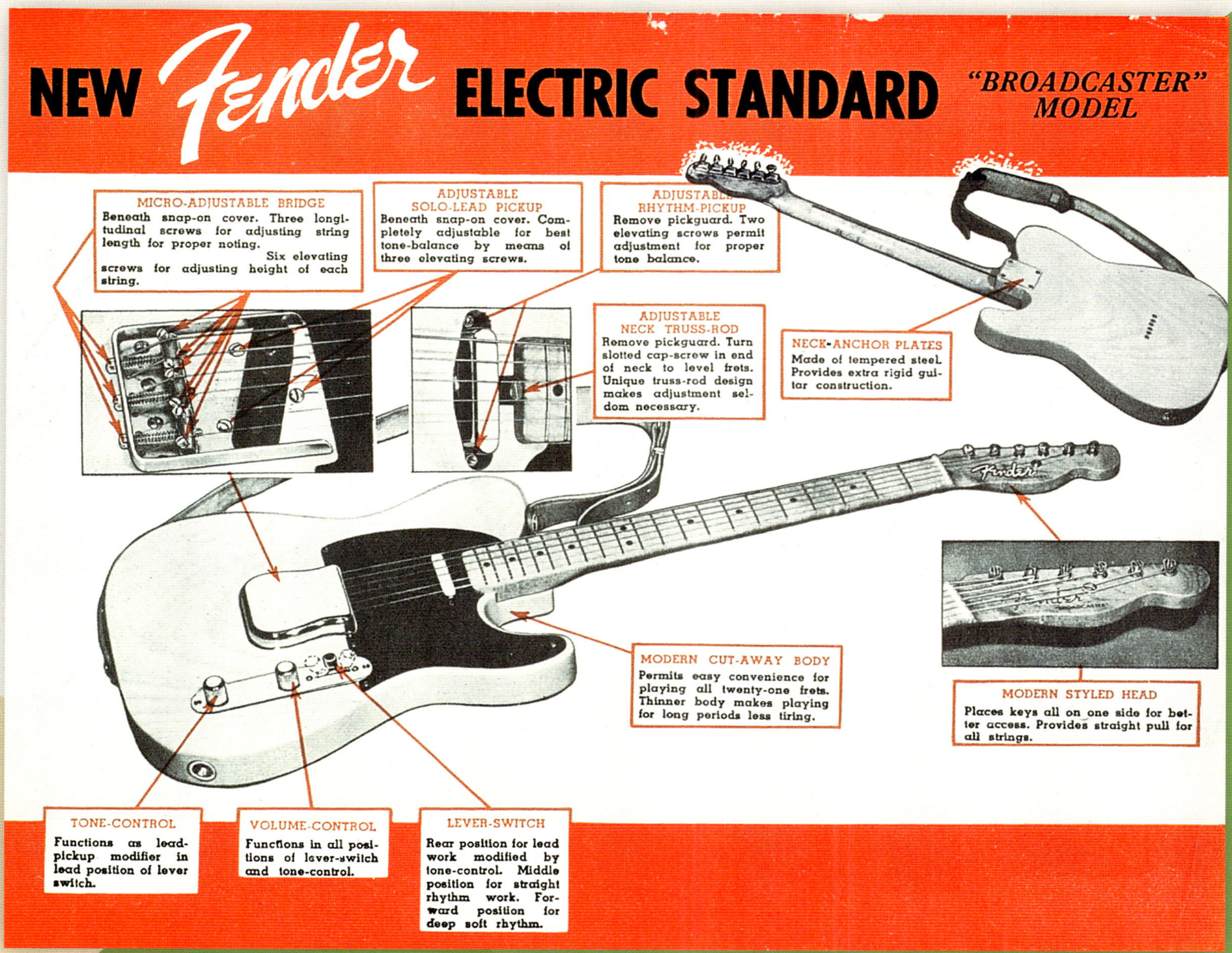

ABOVE: *An early ad for the Broadcaster.*
LEFT: *In 1950 Fender's manufacturing facility gained a new brick building at the corner of Santa Fe and Pomona Avenues, alongside the existing corrugated sheds.*

Chapter 2

IN DEVELOPMENT

MAIN:
Malia Ka'aihue, better known as Mary Kaye, helped invent the Las Vegas lounge genre with her bandmates Frank Ross and Norman Kaye (her brother), pictured here. She was also an early endorser of the Stratocaster.

A Successor to the Telecaster

With his company's debut solidbody electric finding its feet in the market, Leo Fender soon turned his thoughts to developing a follow-up model, one that would address some of the requests he was getting from the many professional guitarists from whom he sought input. Leo said in interviews conducted decades later that he had the basic concept for the new design in place in 1951, and that he alone had already hammered out the basic shape and features.

Considering everything that was already going on that year, though—the year in which Fender dropped the Broadcaster name and scrambled to replace it with Telecaster after a firm request from Gretsch (which felt it was too similar to its "Broadkaster" drum line), and in which the company also developed and released the revolutionary Precision Bass—it seems unlikely he actually got very far along with yet another groundbreaking guitar design that quickly.

(CONTINUED ON PAGE 30)

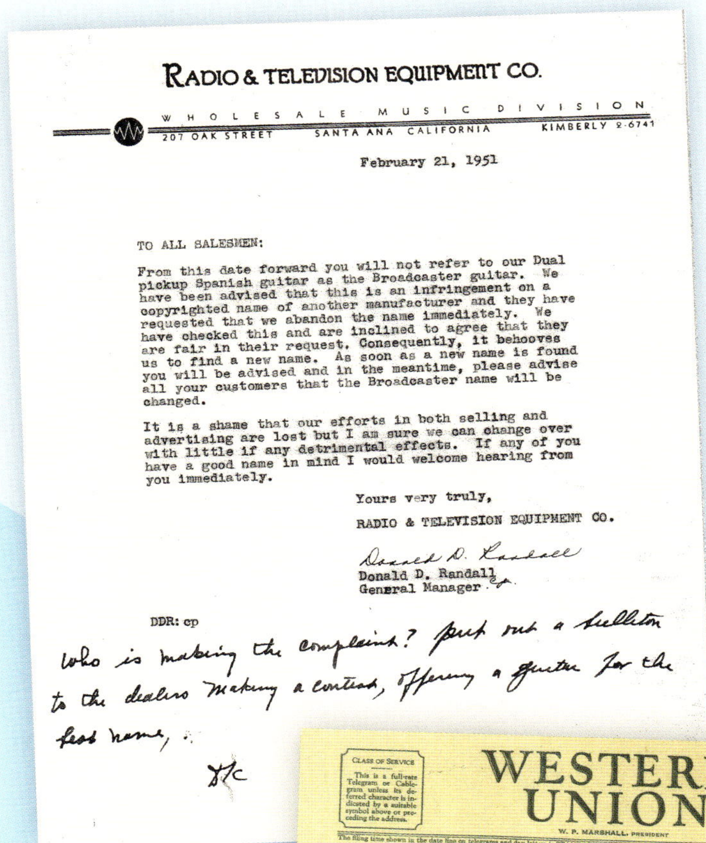

RADIO & TELEVISION EQUIPMENT CO.
WHOLESALE MUSIC DIVISION
207 OAK STREET SANTA ANA CALIFORNIA KIMBERLY 2-6741

February 21, 1951

TO ALL SALESMEN:

From this date forward you will not refer to our Dual pickup Spanish guitar as the Broadcaster guitar. We have been advised that this is an infringement on a copyrighted name of another manufacturer and they have requested that we abandon the name immediately. We have checked this and are inclined to agree that they are fair in their request. Consequently, it behooves us to find a new name. As soon as a new name is found you will be advised and in the meantime, please advise all your customers that the Broadcaster name will be changed.

It is a shame that our efforts in both selling and advertising are lost but I am sure we can change over with little if any detrimental effects. If any of you have a good name in mind I would welcome hearing from you immediately.

Yours very truly,
RADIO & TELEVISION EQUIPMENT CO.

Donald D. Randall
Donald D. Randall
General Manager

DDR: cp

Who is making the complaint? Put out a bulletin to the dealers making a contest, offering a guitar for the best name, etc.

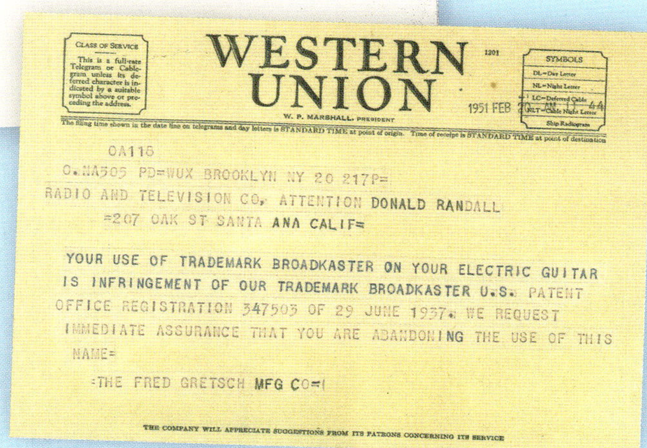

WESTERN UNION
W. P. MARSHALL, PRESIDENT
1951 FEB

OA115
O.NA505 PD=WUX BROOKLYN NY 20 217P=
RADIO AND TELEVISION CO, ATTENTION DONALD RANDALL
=207 OAK ST SANTA ANA CALIF=

YOUR USE OF TRADEMARK BROADKASTER ON YOUR ELECTRIC GUITAR IS INFRINGEMENT OF OUR TRADEMARK BROADKASTER U.S. PATENT OFFICE REGISTRATION 347505 OF 29 JUNE 1937. WE REQUEST IMMEDIATE ASSURANCE THAT YOU ARE ABANDONING THE USE OF THIS NAME=

=THE FRED GRETSCH MFG CO=

THE COMPANY WILL APPRECIATE SUGGESTIONS FROM ITS PATRONS CONCERNING ITS SERVICE

RIGHT TOP:
Don Randall wrote a letter alerting salesmen of the deletion of the Broadcaster name. He included a handwritten note proposing a contest encouraging dealers to submit their suggestions for a new model name.

RIGHT BOTTOM:
The telegram from Gretsch urging Fender to stop using the Broadcaster name.

TOP: *A "Nocaster" headstock from the period between dropping the Broadcaster name and adopting "Telecaster."* **ABOVE:** *An early Telecaster displays the new model name.* **OPPOSITE:** *Two Fender employees test Fender's revolutionary Precision Bass.*

As to the "did it myself" implications, George Fullerton later said that Leo "never gave credit to anybody. There were very few things in my entire life that Leo gave me credit for personally or ever said, 'Hey, you're doing a good job.'"[1]

A broader view of the work that went into the Stratocaster indicates it was likely a team effort that got underway more fully in early 1953, with several individuals playing a role. I've had the pleasure of speaking with Dick over the years (may he rest in peace) and he always spoke of his input to the Strat, as well as the Showman amp. Leo, of course, was very much at the center of it all, but the ultimate recipe for the Stratocaster likely included a pinch of Bill Carson, who started working at Fender in 1951; a dash of Rex Gallion, a local musician who was very vocal about his discomfort with the square-edged Telecaster body; a level table-spoon of sales manager Don Randall; and a heaping cup of Freddie Tavares, the steel-guitar star and gifted engineer who lent his talents to Fender full-time from 1953 onward.

(CONTINUED ON PAGE 34)

ABOVE: *As simple as it appears today, the Precision Bass had a major impact on the sound of popular music.* OPPOSITE: *Fender's patent application for the Precision Bass.* OPPOSITE INSET: *Jazz bassist and early Precision Bass endorser Willie "Shifty" Henry appeared in company ads as "Shifte Henri."*

RICHARD L. GAUSEWITZ
PATENT LAWYER
FIRST WESTERN BANK BLDG.
SANTA ANA, CALIFORNIA

March 24, 1953 — C. L. FENDER — Des. 169,062

GUITAR

Filed Nov. 21, 1952

INVENTOR.
CLARENCE L. FENDER
BY Lyon & Lyon
ATTORNEYS

ABOVE: *The front of the Fender factory on Pomona Avenue in 1952, the new brick building now adorned with the company name.* **OPPOSITE:** *A Fender employee solders amplifier circuits just prior to the Stratocaster's release.*

Freddie Comes to Fender

Leo Fender was first introduced to Freddie Tavares by steel-guitar star Noel Boggs in 1953 during a show with the Ozark Mountain Boys at LA's Cowtown Club. The clincher, it seems, came when Tavares offered several bits of constructive criticism regarding Fender amps of the day—in answer to which Leo Fender pulled out a screwdriver, removed the back panel from Tavares's own homemade amp, checked the work inside the chassis, and offered him a job in the Fender development lab on the spot.[2]

Given Tavares's status in the steel-guitar world, it might seem surprising he would accept the day job at all. He was a busy Hawaiian-steel player who had come to Los Angeles from his birthplace on Maui several years before, landing recording dates with the Andrews Sisters, Deanna Durbin, Dean Martin, Bing Crosby, Sons of the Pioneers, Spike Jones and His City Slickers, and later even Elvis Presley. Even more prominently, Tavares had provided "the *zzziiiing!* heard 'round the world" by recording the iconic slide glissando that opened the *Looney Tunes* theme song. But he was a habitual designer, too, who had taught himself electronics and basic mechanics and designed and built his own steel guitars and amplifiers. The work of the young Fender company was right up his alley, and he took the job and ran with it.

Most reports point to early prototypes of the guitar that would become the Stratocaster looking far more like an evolution of the existing Telecaster. Leo had heard from several musicians who wanted a vibrato unit on a Fender electric, and guitarists Gallion and Carson had voiced their desires for better comfort contours on both the back and front so it wouldn't dig into a player's ribcage and forearm the way the Tele could with extended playing. Most accounts concur, however, that it was Tavares who got right down to business perfecting the shape of the new instrument almost immediately upon his arrival. Fender had just completed a larger new factory on Pomona Street in Fullerton in the spring of 1953, and all the pieces seemed to be in place by that summer for the development of a major new product.

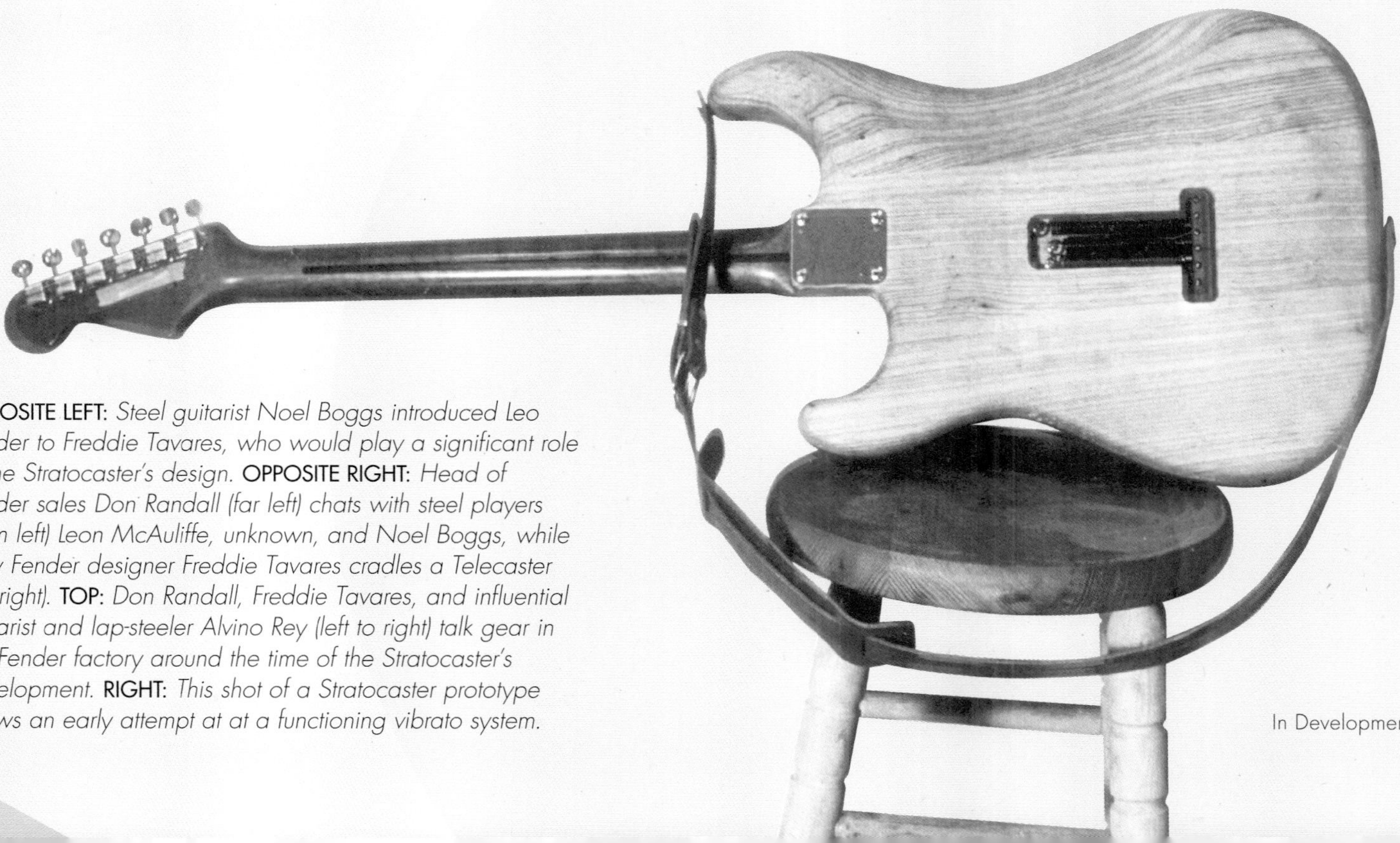

OPPOSITE LEFT: *Steel guitarist Noel Boggs introduced Leo Fender to Freddie Tavares, who would play a significant role in the Stratocaster's design.* **OPPOSITE RIGHT:** *Head of Fender sales Don Randall (far left) chats with steel players (from left) Leon McAuliffe, unknown, and Noel Boggs, while new Fender designer Freddie Tavares cradles a Telecaster (far right).* **TOP:** *Don Randall, Freddie Tavares, and influential guitarist and lap-steeler Alvino Rey (left to right) talk gear in the Fender factory around the time of the Stratocaster's development.* **RIGHT:** *This shot of a Stratocaster prototype shows an early attempt at at a functioning vibrato system.*

VOLUME
TONE
TONE

"The first real project that I had was to put the Stratocaster on [the] drawing board," Tavares later recalled. "It was about April or May 1953 and Leo said, 'We need a new guitar,' and I said, 'How far apart are the strings at the nut, how far [at] the bridge?' I got those parameters and I said, 'What's the scale?' Then I knew where the strings are and we started from there."[3]

The acclaimed guitar-maker John Page worked at Fender from 1978 to 1998 (with a brief hiatus in 1986), enjoying a career that truly spanned the old and the new. He overlapped with Tavares's tenure on the design desk and ultimately rose to be the head of the Custom Shop (we'll explore Page's contributions to Fender further in a following chapter).

Page recalls,

I will always remember what [Freddie] told me he did on the first day working full-time for Leo. He said he went into the shop and grabbed a large piece of plywood. Sanded it until it was incredibly smooth, then drew two lines that were exactly twenty-five and one-half inches apart. Those two lines became the first drawing of the Stratocaster.

When I asked him about his role in designing the Strat and how it felt to have designed the most famous guitar in the world, he shrugged off any credit. He said that every line he drew had to be approved by Leo, so he felt Leo deserved all the credit. That was his humility talking. I know, as a designer, how much of himself must've gone into the design. But he gave all the credit to his friend and boss, Leo Fender.[4]

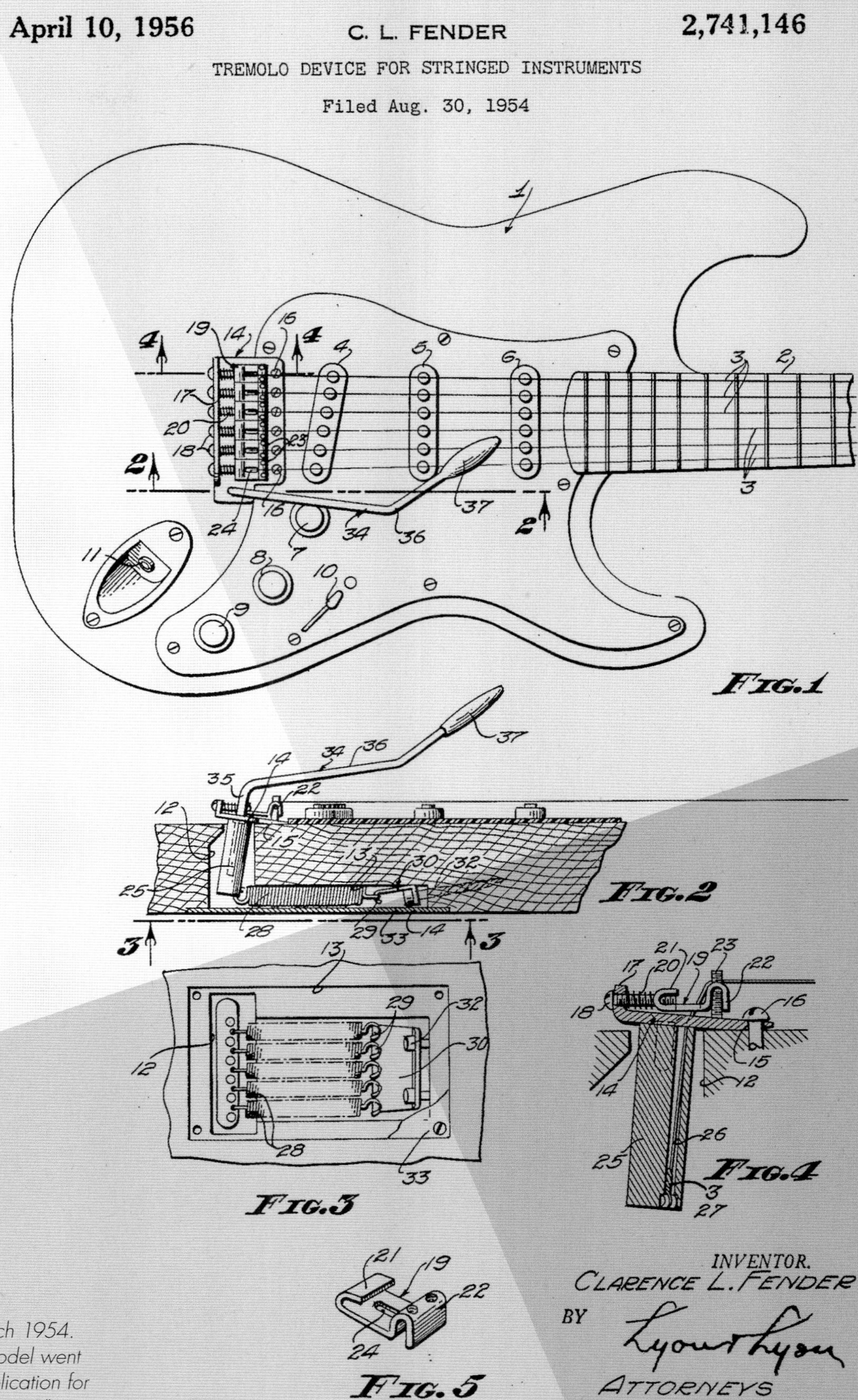

OPPOSITE: *A rare Stratocaster prototype built in March 1954. Most prototype guitars were destroyed before the model went into production.* RIGHT: *The August 1954 patent application for the Stratocaster's "Tremolo Device for Stringed Instruments."*

LEFT: *Bill Carson was an early proponent and test pilot of the new Stratocaster.*
OPPOSITE: *The deep comfort contours on the back of an early "pre-production" 1954 Stratocaster.*

The now-legendary body shape was derived from the basic asymmetrical double-cutaway lines of the existing Precision Bass, made far sleeker, rounder, and more stylish with careful use of the bandsaw and sanding belt. In addition to its undeniable visual appeal, Tavares's design also suited playing ergonomics to a T. Bill Carson recalls having tested prototypes earlier in '53 that already carried roughed-out ribcage and forearm contours, but they didn't balance well or hang quite right on the strap. Tavares's design not only cured those ills but also defined one of the most comfortably playable guitars that has ever been created.

More than just an ergonomic fit, the elegantly thrusting yet rounded asymmetrical double-cutaway shape that Freddie, Leo, and the team created established one of the most timelessly artful pieces of design in any industry. "When I first saw a Stratocaster properly I realized that it's a thing of sculpted beauty," said Mark Knopfler. "If you look at the cross section, I mean, that could be something flying through space, to me. It's a utilitarian thing, but it's beautiful."[5] Name another achievement in product design of seventy years ago—or even fifty or sixty—that still looks as sharp, fresh, and vital today without falling back on "retro" or "throwback" to bolster its appeal. It's not easily done.

"No kids are saying: 'What's that old guitar, ain't you got a new one?'" said Jeff Beck. "It still looks futuristic, still an unbeatable shape, as is the Tele. I don't think you can improve on those two guitars, the all-time great rock guitars."[6]

The Pieces Come Together

Fender already had the template in place for pickups that would faithfully reproduce what was coming to be known as "the Fender sound," but it's interesting to note that Leo never used exactly the same pickups on two different models of guitar, even if the basic ingredients were much the same. All of Fender's pickups of the 1950s and 1960s used six individual Alnico rod magnets secured between two fiber plates with a coil of wire wound around them, but from there they varied in size and shape. Why not simply port a version of the Telecaster bridge pickup over to the new design? It's difficult to say, but of course Leo was a design fiend who thrived at the workbench with soldering iron in hand. Perhaps the temptation to concoct yet another good pickup was just too difficult to resist.

As previously noted, Fender pickups were already known for their clear, crisp sound and excellent string-to-string articulation, and these qualities were carried forward to the new model. To further enhance the string-to-string balance, Fender also used magnets of staggered heights on the new Stratocaster pickups, with lower magnets on the louder strings for a comparable overall output across all six.

The inclusion of three of these new pickups on the new guitar also proved a feature the sales team could brag about, and the trio sure looked impressive up against what was available in the day. Even if the three pickups didn't give the Stratocaster, with its three-way switch, any more tonal selections than the Telecaster already possessed, those it did have were arguably already more usable: right from the start, the Strat avoided the unpopular preset "bassy sound" that the Telecaster was wired to produce from the neck pickup in the forward switch position.

In addition, the positioning of the three-way switch and three controls was arguably more ergonomic than that of any production electric guitar seen before, with the single master volume control very consciously positioned within reach of the player's right-hand "pinky" finger for easy volume swells. Clever players quickly discovered that even more could be done to enhance the guitar's versatility than was allowed by the original switching mechanism. For its day, even selecting each of the three pickups individually represented quite a feature. And those players who figured out how to balance the three-way switch *between* the 1 and 2 and 2 and 3 positions were rewarded with a total of five distinct tones, something Fender would officially adopt several years later with a five-position switch.

Despite Fender's established prowess in pickup design, field-tester Bill Carson indicated some early dissatisfaction with the units in a prototype Stratocaster that was likely completed around mid-1953—although this verdict might have come out of some misinterpretation of the problem.

"One of the early failures we had were the first pickups," he told Tom Wheeler in an interview for *Guitar Player* magazine. "They just didn't make it. I don't know what happened, but they seemed to lose a lot between when Leo made them at the shop and when I took them out on the job. The sound had a rapid decay and a somewhat banjo-like tone."[7]

Given Leo's well-established ability to wind a robust pickup, there's a good chance this poor sustain and pingy "banjo-like" tone was coming from another failing within the design as a whole, one that would in fact hold up the final release of the Stratocaster by several months.

THIS PAGE: *In 1954, the Stratocaster's three pickups, three control knobs, and three-way switch represented unprecedented sonic versatility.* **OPPOSITE:** *Inside and underside looks at the pickups of an early 1954 Stratocaster.*

Tremol-No

The vibrato bridge planned for the Stratocaster, the first from Fender, was intended to be a doozy, and the effort put into its design drained a considerable amount of the R&D team's man hours. It appears an early design was well underway before Tavares brought his considerable engineering chops to the team, but the gulf between conception and function for this early effort was apparently too broad to span. In later interviews, George Fullerton recalled that the final Stratocaster vibrato was the last piece of the puzzle to come together and that the failing of the first completed attempt found Fender missing its anticipated release window, intended to coincide with an unveiling at the summer NAMM (National Association of Music Merchants) show of 1953.

Some one hundred units were on their way through the assembly line in mid-1953, and Fullerton tested one completed guitar coming off the other end. "I grabbed that one and tested it out," said Fullerton, "and it was terribly bad sounding. . . . I rushed to the lab, Leo and I looked at it, and we called Freddie over to look at it. That vibrato sounded like a tin can. We all agreed it wasn't going to work, so we shut down the line. It was a sad day. It was then that Leo went back to the drawing board."[8]

Multiple accounts indicate that the first effort at a functioning vibrato for the Stratocaster resulted in something that more closely resembled the "floating tremolo" system eventually used in the Jazzmaster of 1958, yet it clearly lacked the final refinements that would help make that later piece of hardware a success. (Note that Fender incorrectly used the term *tremolo* for *vibrato* throughout these years. Genuine tremolo produces a fluctuation in volume, whereas vibrato produces a fluctuation in pitch, which is what both the Stratocaster and Jazzmaster "tremolos" achieve.) The flaw in the early design of 1953, however, appeared to be a lack of mass at the strings' body-end termination point, which resulted in a thin sound and poor sustain.

To correct these failings, Leo, Tavares, and the team devised a steel inertia block that he mounted below the vibrato's baseplate. The strings were loaded into holes drilled through the block and, as a result, were anchored with the mass needed for satisfactory tone and sustain.

The rejig put the Stratocaster's development back by as much as six months, but it yielded a genuine wonder of engineering. The new unit, dubbed the "Synchronized Tremolo" in Fender's catalog lingo, was light years ahead of the existing Bigsby and Kauffman vibratos for both design virtuosity and advanced function: it allowed for deep bends and gentle vibrato-like flutters alike, with excellent tuning stability. Playing comfort was good—aided by a small, elegant metal cover that many players removed and used as an ashtray—and the free-swinging arm enabled myriad styles and hand positions. The unit also provided pinpoint intonation accuracy courtesy of its six individually adjustable string saddles, and it did all of the above without adversely affecting the guitar's overall tone.

While countless guitarists agree that the Stratocaster was an impressively well-integrated design, for many it's the achievement represented by the new vibrato bridge that really pushed the guitar over the top as an expressive and inspiring instrument.

"The vibrato—it's like the gear stick on a car, you have to have it," said Jeff Beck. "I jammed with Eric [Clapton] once and unbeknownst to me, he handed me his Strat, the black one he uses, and I think he has the vibrato arm glued down. He never dreamt of using it. And I think with the Strat, that's the beauty of it. The tonal flexibility of that bar: you can play a phrase and lower it and raise it and wang it. It becomes a whole different ball game with that on."[9]

TOP: *An early 1954 Stratocaster's back cavity reveals the springs that enable its vibrato's function.* **BOTTOM:** *The Stratocaster's vibrato design was groundbreaking.*

Even with all that to boast about, the Fender team continues to pile thoughtful features into the effort. Today we're so familiar with the Stratocaster's recessed, angled, top-mounted jack that we're likely to give little thought to what an elegant and utilitarian piece of design it truly is, but this little rocket-shaped bit of metal single-handedly put an end to the plague of cracked jack mountings that other guitars suffered when players stepped on their guitar cords and inadvertently yanked the things out. Don Randall himself apparently lobbied for the larger headstock—somewhere between the svelte Telecaster headstock shape and the more curvaceous scroll used by Paul Bigsby on his Merle Travis guitars—as a canvas on which to more prominently display the Fender logo. And Leo, Don, and others apparently agreed that the new guitar should be painted in a sunburst finish, giving it a more regal and traditional look befitting an upmarket instrument.

TOP: *The headstock of the 1954 Stratocaster was a graceful enlargement of the six-a-side Telecaster headstock.* ABOVE: *The inset, angled jack plate was another subtle but highly practical innovation of the Stratocaster design.* OPPOSITE: *This "pre-production" 1954 Stratocaster displays the sunburst finish that would be standard on the model.*

Fender Sales, Inc.

Meanwhile, just about the time the would-be Stratocaster vibrato bridge was headed back to the R&D department, Fender was undergoing a major shake-up of the department that would play a big part in bringing the new model to the public's attention. Although he was still technically the general manager of Fender distributor Radio-Tel, Don Randall was a partner in Fender in all but name. It was Randall who had urged Leo Fender to include a truss rod in the early Broadcaster and who had coined the new Telecaster model name after Gretsch's cease-and-desist letter. He and the sales team had also made myriad suggestions regarding features and USPs that would aid the reps' efforts to get a foot in the door at music stores around the country. Add all this to the fact that Leo and Radio-Tel owner F. C. Hall had begun to fall out around this time, and things were ripe for a change.

In June 1953, Fender terminated its contract with Radio-Tel for exclusive representation of its products, and Randall left his position as Radio-Tel's general manager. Leo Fender and Don Randall formed Fender Sales, Inc., of which Randall was made president while also becoming a partner in Fender Electronic Instruments itself.

Amid all the talk of who-designed-this and who-requested-that regarding the Stratocaster's development, it's worth remembering that the man responsible for selling Fender instruments, and the team working under him, played an enormous part in the feedback network between player, dealer, and maker.

For all his undoubted contribution to the effort, though, perhaps the biggest element of the new model for which Randall is widely credited is its name. His Telecaster model name took the company's debut solidbody from the radio age into the television age, and the sales manager—a licensed pilot and avid flyer—would take the new model even further with his next moniker.

"It wasn't easy," Randall would later tell author Tony Bacon. "I tried to maintain a family reference. For instance, we had the Broadcaster, we put it on the market. . . . About that time, television was getting big, so telecast—Telecaster! And then when the Stratocaster came along, why, they were talking about putting guys into orbit, so Telecaster, then Stratocaster into the stratosphere."[10]

LEFT: *When Don Randall formed Fender Sales Inc. with Leo Fender, he was also made president and became a partner in Fender Electronic Instruments itself.* **OPPOSITE:** *An "exploded" view of the new Stratocaster.*

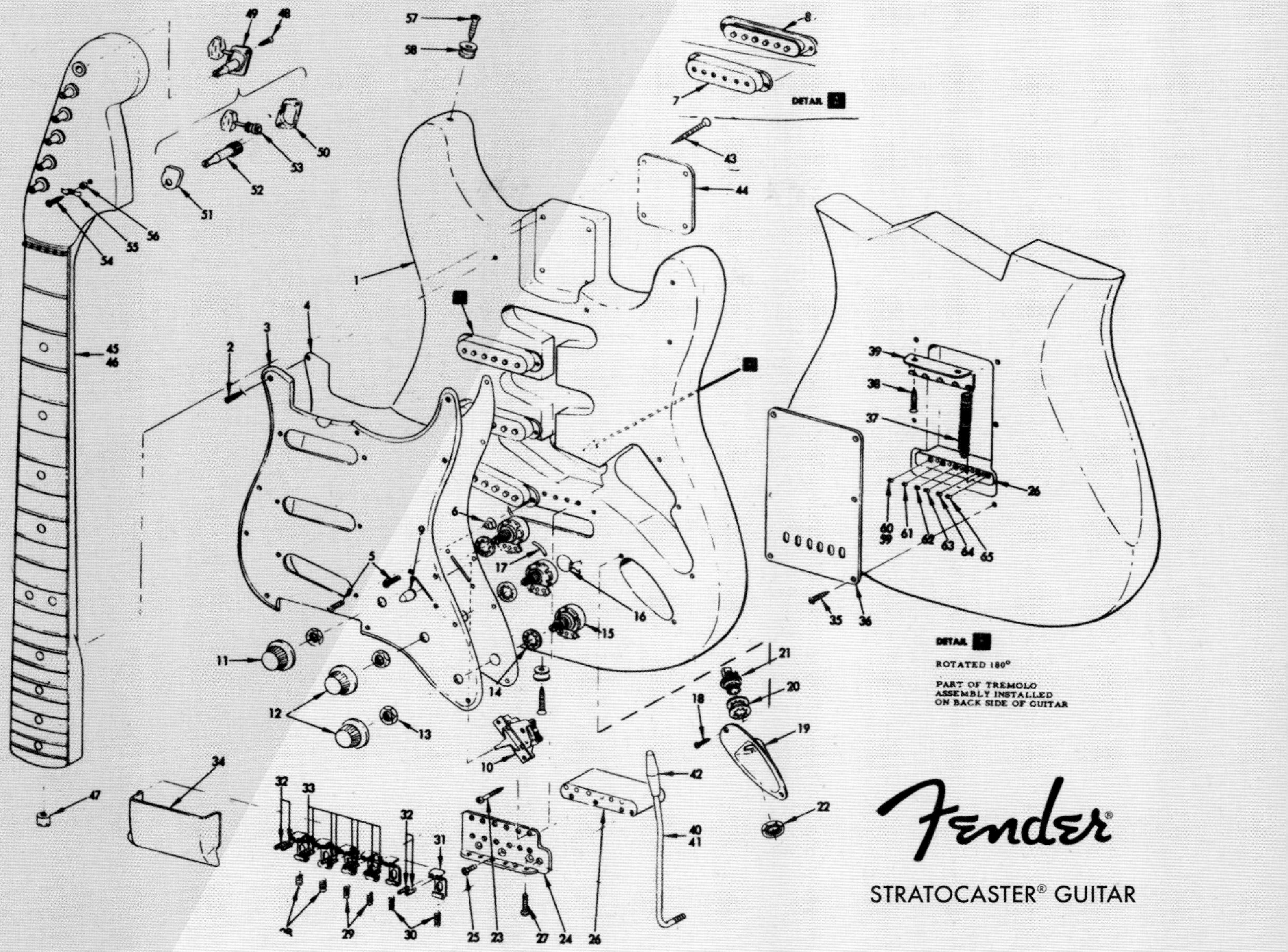

Prototypes Hit the Streets

Sales guys being sales guys, Randall obviously would have preferred that the Stratocaster come along quicker, certainly in time for the summer NAMM show of 1953 as originally anticipated. But in hindsight he probably would have agreed that it paid to get it right. Most accounts indicate that Fender had working prototypes in the field even before the end of that year regardless of the holdup with the Synchronized Tremolo. If Randall, Fullerton, and others later asserted that Bill Carson had less to do with the design of the new guitar than he himself might occasionally have claimed, there's no doubt that he remained a valued test pilot. Given Leo Fender's propensity to field comments from working musicians, there were likely other test units passed around, but existing prototypes are extremely hard to come by.

In his book *Fender: The Sound Heard 'Round the World*, Richard Smith published photos taken by Leo Fender of a supposed Stratocaster prototype from 1953 that showed a "breadboard" guitar of sorts, with a black fiber pickguard, knurled silver Telecaster-style knobs, and a back route wide enough to take only three springs rather than the standard five.[11] Aside from that, however, Stratocaster prototypes are thin on the ground, to say the least. And according to George Fullerton, there was good reason for that: "Leo Fender was the type of person, soon as a prototype was proven, you'd cut it up and get rid of it, you won't keep it around any longer. So most of the prototypes got cut up and thrown away."[12]

Whatever the fate of the several prototypes that were likely handed round the Fender factory for testing, there's little doubt that the final-spec Stratocaster was in place and ready for manufacturing by the end of 1953 or the very start of 1954. It would be some months yet until the general public would get its hands on this revolutionary new creation, but guitars that are entirely recognizable today as Stratocaster guitars were coming out of Fullerton by March 1954. It's fair to say that by midsummer of that year, the guitar industry was getting wind of a new electric solidbody that would forever change the look and feel of the instrument.

Stratocaster endorsers across a variety of genres appeared pleased with the revolutionary new instrument.

STASH CLEMENTS
PREFERS
Fender
FINE ELECTRIC INSTRUMENTS

ALVINO REY
prefers
Fender
Fine Electric Instruments

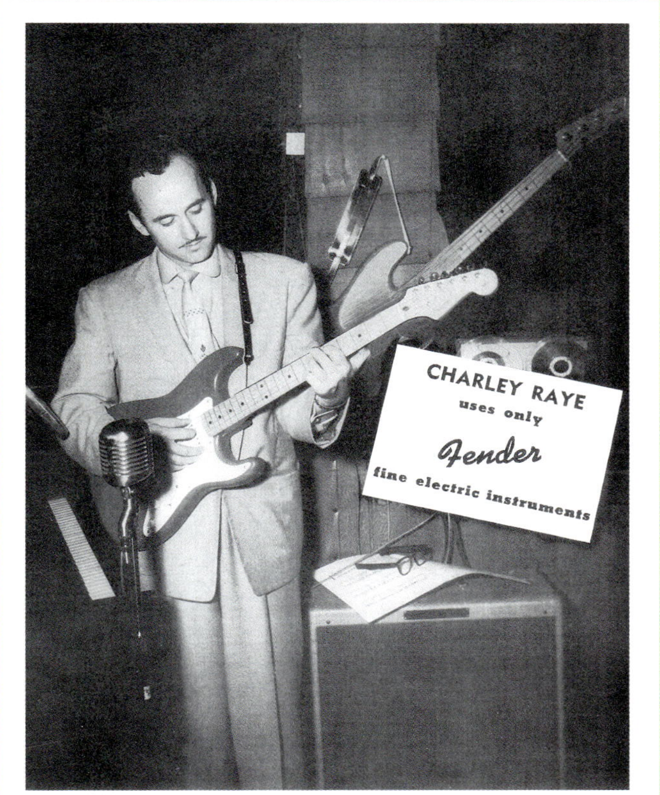
CHARLEY RAYE
uses only
Fender
fine electric instruments

AL MYERS
prefers
Fender FINE ELECTRIC INSTRUMENTS
FENDER

Chapter

3

THE STRATOCASTER IS HERE

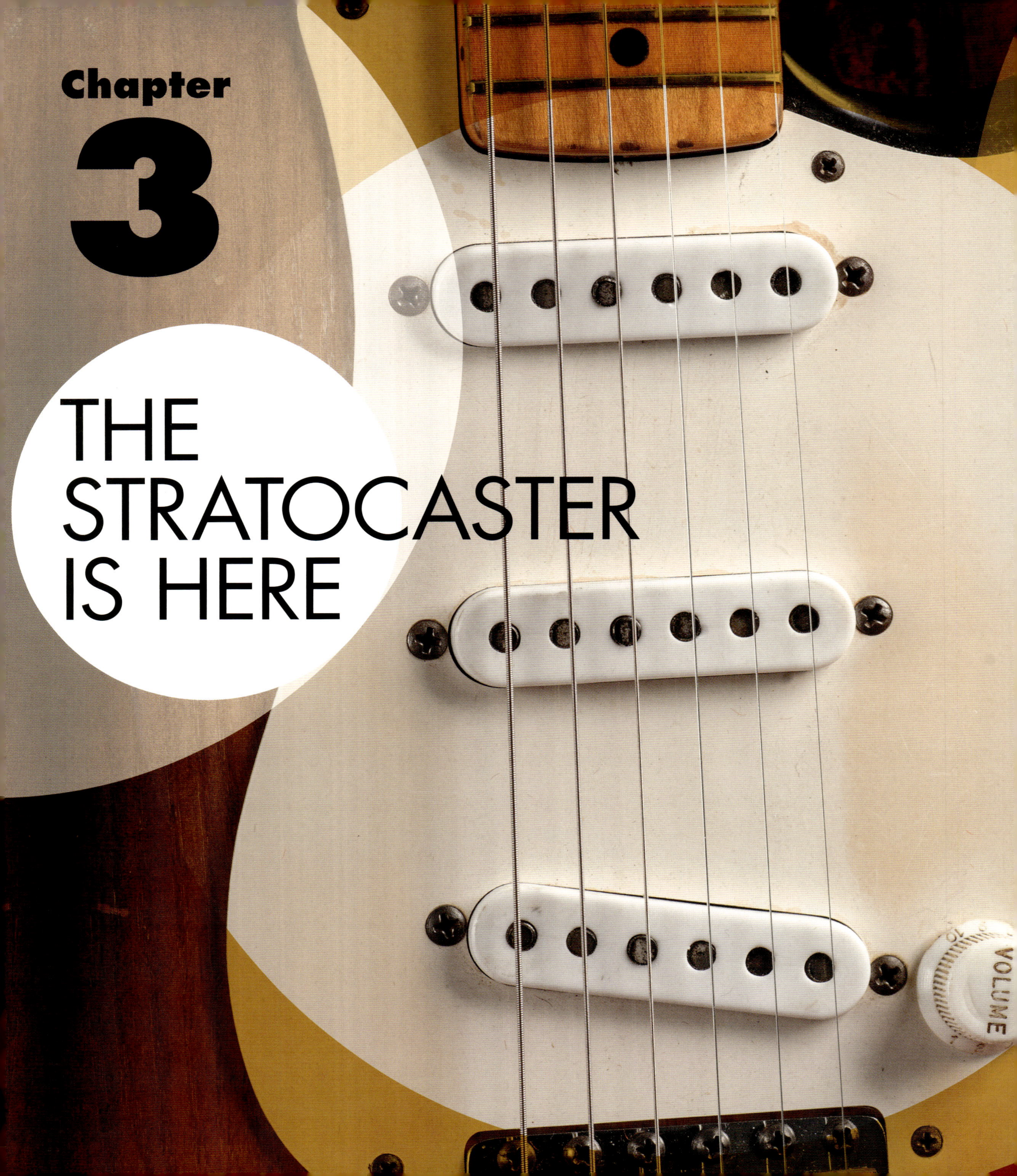

"First again in the field of amplified music . . ." Proper production-run Stratocasters reached market around October 1954.

Priming for Production

Following intensive testing, prototyping, and the necessary redrawing of the vibrato bridge design, early versions of what would become the production Stratocaster guitars finally saw the light of day around March 1954. At the time, Fender sales literature announced that "shipments are expected to begin May 15," but that appears to have been optimistic. Release deadlines being what they were, proper production-run Strats didn't reach the public until around October 1954, a timeline which has led many historians to refer to guitars made in the spring and summer of that year as "pre-production" Stratocaster guitars.

Even so, the model had already been announced and was being featured in the Fender catalog and trade advertisements, and no major identifying changes were made to specifications between the guitars made in the summer and those that followed in more plentiful numbers in the fall, aside from some details regarding serial number placement and sequencing and plastics formulations. So we might also consider these to be "early production models."

(CONTINUED ON PAGE 57)

ABOVE: *An early "pre-production" Stratocaster from May, 1954.* OPPOSITE: *Note the "5-54" neck date. The initials "TG" indicate Tadeo Gomez, a noted builder of early Fender necks.*

LEFT: *An early 1954 "pre-production" Stratocaster with tremolo-plate serial #0108.* **RIGHT:** *"Pre-production" 1954 Stratocaster with trem-cover serial #0189.* **OPPOSITE:** *An early production Stratocaster from late-summer or fall of 1954 with neck-plate serial number.*

Fender

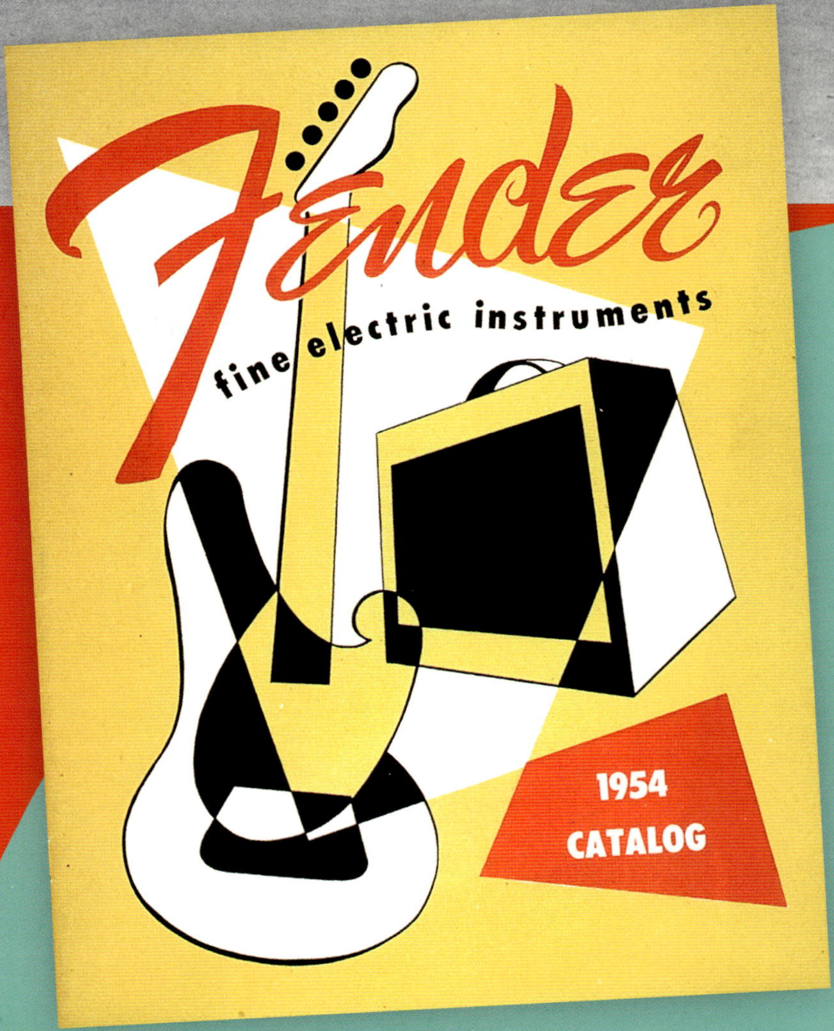

ABOVE: *Final assembly, tuning, setup, and testing of Stratocasters in 1954.* RIGHT: *The cover of Fender's 1954 catalog features a stylized take on the soon-to-be iconic shape.* OPPOSITE: *A Stratocaster ad from 1954 touts the "comfort contoured" body.*

The Sum of Its Parts

Early Fender ads for the new Stratocaster went out of their way to declare the benefits of the new model, while hinting heavily at the futuristic nature of the design:

First again in the field of amplified music . . . the thrilling new "Stratocaster" by Fender!

It's engineered to fit the artist's body . . . designed to be "part of the player."

See the new, revolutionary Fender Stratocaster at your dealer soon . . . play it . . . and be the first to experience this new amplified music thrill!

Years ahead in design—unequalled in performance . . . a flick of the wrist means live, tremolo action—perfect pitch. You've a new thrill in store for you when you play this revolutionary new instrument. Three separate pick-ups, a special tone control circuit, a new surface mounted plug receptacle all mean faster action, better, clearer music . . . whether you play it "straight" or while using the revolutionary Tremolo Action lever. The Stratocaster features advanced design in body too! Here is an instrument actually "comfort contoured" for you!

At the time of its launch, the Stratocaster's retail price was set at $249.50 with Synchronized Tremolo or $229.50 in the "hardtail" version without the vibrato, plus $39.95 for the case (the Telecaster was $189.50). If these prices send you racing to the drawing board to finally invent that time machine, it's worth pointing out that the cost of the average house in 1954 was $10,250, a new car averaged $1,700, and average yearly wages were $4,100, so a new electric guitar from one of the nation's most popular up-and-coming makers was by no means a cheap proposition. By comparison, a 1954 Gibson Les Paul "goldtop" listed for $225, while a Gretsch Duo Jet from around the same time cost $290.

After all the input regarding desirable features for the new model and the somewhat rushed, stumbling-toward-perfection nature of the prototyping process, a mere list of the significant design points that this very new style of electric guitar presented gives a more detailed look and can help us fathom just what a "revolutionary new instrument" it really was. Notable features of the new model included the following:

- Larger headstock, purportedly requested by Don Randall to better display the Fender logo
- More comfortable body shape, with contours where it met the player's ribcage and right forearm
- Broader sonic range, courtesy of three individual pickups routed through a three-way switch, two tone controls, and a master volume control
- More ergonomic control layout, along with a recessed jack for accidental pull-out safety
- Built-in vibrato bridge with six bridge saddles individually adjustable for height and length (a first among large-scale-production guitars)
- Two-tone Sunburst finish as standard
- Stylish, ultra-modern looks

LEFT: *Final assembly, tuning, setup, and testing of Stratocasters in 1954.* OPPOSITE: *Some of the Stratocaster's novel features—including its vibrato bridge; angled, recessed jack plate; control layout; contoured body; and trio of pickups—were truly a leap forward in electric guitar design and functionality.*

VOLUME
TONE
TONE

TONE
TONE
VOLUME

If these basic ingredients are all very familiar today, it might take some reconfiguring of our perspective to fully perceive just how radical this instrument was that hit an unsuspecting music world in mid-1954. With countless Strat-a-likes available today in the form of everything from sub-$100 imports to $10,000 Custom Shop and luthier-grade re-creations, it can be difficult to comprehend quite how *new* the Stratocaster appeared in 1954 and what its impact was, both in look and in tone. This was a world that needed the Fender Stratocaster, even if it didn't yet know it. Before it came along, there was nothing remotely like it, either in the music world or in pop culture in general.

Let's consider for a moment the world into which this radical new instrument was born. The early Cold War era saw both the economy and popular culture booming in the United States, yet in 1954 so many of the revolutionary cultural and commercial developments that were commonplace by the end of the decade had yet to make their impact. Here are highlights of the 1954 into which the Stratocaster arrived:

- The US Navy launched its first nuclear submarine.
- Hydrogen bomb tests were in full swing on Bikini Atoll in the Pacific Ocean.
- The first organ transplants were carried out in hospitals in Boston and Paris.
- *Brown v. Board of Education* made segregation in US public schools illegal.
- British runner Roger Bannister clocked the first under-four-minute mile.
- NBC's *The Tonight Show* first aired, with host Steve Allen.
- Marlon Brando starred in two major hit movies, *On the Waterfront* and *The Wild Ones*.
- America's first jet airliner, the Boeing 707, makes its maiden flight.
- Swanson sold its first TV dinner.
- The term *rock 'n' roll* began to enter the lexicon, thanks in part to the release of the movie *Blackboard Jungle*, featuring "Rock Around the Clock" by Bill Haley and the Comets.
- Elvis Presley launched his recording career.

And amid all of this, the Fender Stratocaster soared forth—startling, radical, stylish, and entirely awe-inspiring, even in this fast-paced, future-now age. Yet for all its potential and invention, the Stratocaster didn't set the guitar world on fire overnight. The guitar market has always represented relatively conservative tastes, and in 1954 Fender was still striving for acceptance among the bigger and more traditional names in the industry. The company that had just landed the most radical and revolutionary musical instrument ever presented to the music community was yet something of an upstart, just eight years into its existence.

With all this in mind, it's worth noting that other similarly futuristic guitar designs have often been slow to achieve acceptance with a wary buying public. Even in the rock 'n' roll hotbed of the late 1950s, Gibson's now-iconic Flying V and Explorer were given the cold shoulder, and the final iteration of the Les Paul of 1958–1960 sold so poorly that it was essentially deleted from the catalog and revamped into the entirely different SG body style. Within that context we have to consider the Stratocaster's slow-burn acceptance a success of sorts. And if it wasn't selling off guitar-store racks in droves upon its arrival, it did at least gain steady traction through its early days and was clearly marked as a classic not long into its existence. Consider, too, that the Telecaster and Stratocaster were the only true solidbodies from a major maker to survive through the 1950s, 1960s, and beyond without being majorly redesigned or dropped from the catalog altogether, and you can begin to fathom the impressive staying power of Fender's seminal creations.

The Stratocaster was born into a year of seismic social and cultural events, including nuclear testing on the Bikini Atoll, the emergence of Elvis Presley, the maiden flight of America's first jetliner, and the landmark Brown vs Board of Education *case.*

A Deeper Dive

While it might be relatively easy to slap together a bundle of unique new features and call a guitar "revolutionary," if each of these fails to provide genuine benefits to tone and performance, the resultant instrument is likely to be a flash in the pan and a commercial failure. The features of the Stratocaster that hit the ground running in 1954 have already been checked off, and the sonic contributions of the pickups and the Synchronized Tremolo (vibrato bridge) were discussed in some depth in chapters 1 and 2, so let's take a closer look at how some of the other foundational components, design parameters, and structural elements contribute to the Stratocaster's unique personality.

Solid Ash or Alder Body

The entire Fender ethos for the electric guitar was founded on the solid-wood body, to the extent that it can be a little difficult to contemplate Fender guitars in general without assuming this element. Even so, its contribution to the tonal formula can't be ignored. Aside from the sonic properties of the common tonewoods used in Stratocaster bodies (further explored below, and again in the following chapter), the construction of a guitar with a slab-styled body made from one or two pieces of the same wood, with minimal use of glue and lack of adornments, produces a different sonic foundation than a guitar made with a hollow or semihollow body, or with laminates of different types of woods.

Quantifying such factors can be tricky, but suffice it to say that such a design allows a relatively unencumbered vibration of the wood itself, and since there is only one species involved, it presents the pure characteristics of that type of wood without the hybrid nature of multiwood constructions or heavy adornments to assess. What we *can* say is that this approach to construction enhances the Stratocaster's clarity and tonal purity, which is further emphasized by other elements of the design. But it certainly begins from the ground up with the solid-wood body.

The Stratocaster has mainly been associated with two types of tonewood: production models were born with swamp ash bodies and retained them for the first few years of the guitar's existence, while alder became the wood of standard models a few years later (a transition discussed in chapter 5). The tonal magic of a good piece of swamp ash is largely attributable to the porosity of the wood, a result of the conditions in which it grows. Timber growing below or near the surface of a swamp or wetland absorbs greater quantities of water than higher parts of the tree, which causes the pores to swell. As the wood dries, these pores empty of water, leaving myriad tiny air pockets in a wood that is nevertheless strong and workable.

"Generally speaking," says Chris Fleming, a former master builder with the Fender Custom Shop, "ash can have a warm, round sound, with a bit of a focused cut to it. It can also be, depending on the guitar, a bit shrill, a bit snarly." As a result, such guitars are "very rich, they're very loud, and they cut through a band very well."[1]

While many players today closely associate wood species with guitar models, it's unlikely that the sonic characteristics of any particular timber figured into Leo Fender's thinking while seeking quantities of wood to work with, or at least as long as that wood was workable and didn't result in guitars that sounded demonstrably bad. "Being a very frugal and production-minded guy," Fleming added, "he looked for woods that he could get cheaply and sustainably. At that time ash was a good candidate."

Regarding the shift to alder a few years later, Fleming reasons, "I think it was more important to have a steady source of acceptable-quality wood to put into their products, and one of the main reasons that they went to alder was that it was probably cheaper and more readily available."

Even so, alder does have slightly different sonic characteristics than swamp ash. This is generally heard as a strong, clear, full-bodied, and well-balanced sound, often with more prominent mids, warm lows, and sweet highs. While many players and collectors seem to have romanticized swamp ash as the foundational golden-age Fender tonewood, it's important to note that a good builder can create a Stratocaster capable of achieving a wide palette of tones regardless of the wood used to make its body. And when we consider that Jimi Hendrix, Stevie Ray Vaughan, Eric Clapton, Ritchie Blackmore, and many other Strat stars did the majority of their playing on alder-bodied guitars, such biased distinctions between alder and swamp ash tend to go out the window.

(CONTINUED ON PAGE 66)

Earlier Stratocaster bodies made with ash (this page) often reveal a more distinctive grain than that seen on the alder (next spread) that followed.

TONE

A 1954 Stratocaster's maple neck with integral maple fingerboard.

Scale Length: 25½"

Whether Leo Fender settled on the Telecaster's (and therefore, Stratocaster's) scale length by happy accident or by conscious design, it certainly worked toward achieving his goals for the instruments. According to Forrest White, who was hired by Leo in 1954 as factory manager and eventually rose to be vice president of Fender, "Leo told me the scale and fret placement had been copied from a Gretsch archtop guitar. This is why it was 25½ inches [64.8 cm] from the nut to the bridge."[2]

Many other popular guitars of the day, several Gibsons included, used slightly shorter scale lengths of approximately 24¾" [62.9 cm], but the 25½" [64.8 cm] scale—which would follow on the Stratocaster and Jazzmaster—enhanced the bright, shimmering response that Fender was chasing in the first place while helping to retain a bold, tight low end on the wound strings, both of which have become archetypes of the Fender sound.

In his presentation to the 1995 convention of the Guild of American Luthiers, guitar-maker Ralph Novak said that of all factors that affect a guitar's tone, "scale length comes first because the harmonic content of the final tone produced by the instrument begins with the string. Factors such as structure and materials can only act as 'filters' to tone; they can't add anything, they only modify input. Therefore, if the harmonic structure is not present in the string tone, it won't exist in the final tone."

Suffice it to say that scale length is a cornerstone of design for any thoughtful maker and one of the first major choices to be made when conceiving the voice of an instrument. The fact that Leo Fender settled on the 25½" [64.8 cm] scale seems perhaps to have been serendipitous, but the choice served to emphasize many of the other sonic characteristics he was hoping to achieve with this guitar.

Bolt-on Neck

The fact that the archetypal Fender electric guitar has always been made with a neck attached with four wood screws (erroneously called "*bolt*-on") has become one of the defining factors of the company's approach to construction. For some players, particularly in the early days of Fender's struggle for acceptance, this method was seen as "cheaper," a form of cost savings, although it's just as easy—and arguably even more cost-effective—to squirt some glue into a neck pocket and clamp the neck in place until it sets.

The bolt-on neck does yield some savings in labor in that it's generally easier to align and adjust, and that latter point speaks to one of Leo Fender's main criteria for his creations: they should be easy and affordable to manufacture and also *repair*. A neck attached with wood screws is a lot easier to repair or replace than one that is glued to the guitar's body.

In addition to issues regarding manufacture and repair, however, most thoughtful guitar makers agree that a bolt-on neck contributes its own sonic characteristics to the overall recipe of any given guitar. While a well-cut and tightly fitted screwed-on neck joint can be just as snug and secure as any glued joint, the neck and body woods in this scenario are considered to remain just the slightest bit decoupled due to the presence of tiny air gaps between the two surfaces, natural inconsistencies in wood grain, dimples, or irregularities in the finish, and other minute voids that would be filled with glue in a glued-in neck joint.

Some sonic characteristics resulting from this slight decoupling can include a certain percussive "snap" and "spank" heard in the guitar's sound, a more clearly defined sense of pick attack in the note, and an increase in the bright, shimmery characteristics that we tend to think of as "jangle" or "chime"—which is to say, all the classic components of the Stratocaster sound, and the sound of other seminal Fender electric guitars, for that matter.

The so-called "bolt-on" neck—actually attached with four wood screws—as in the inset photo—is a big part of the Fender constructional DNA.

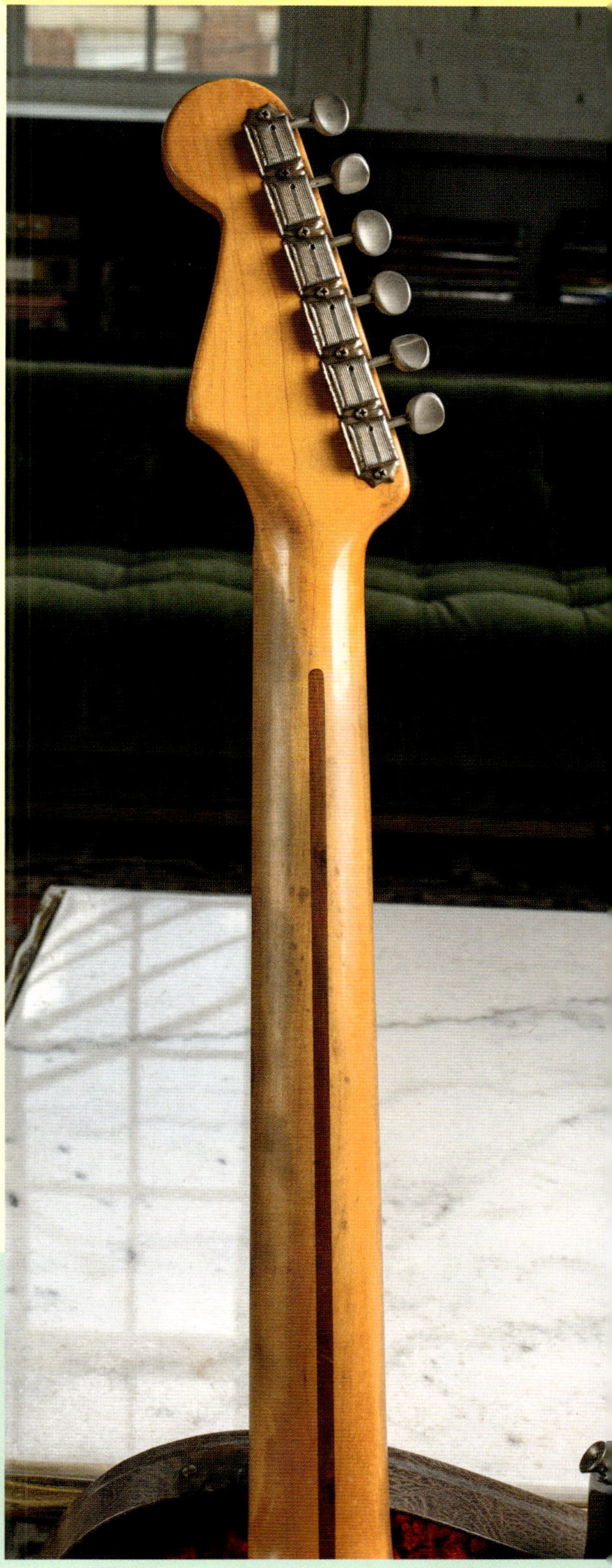

Chapter

4

EVOLUTION THROUGH THE '50S

A Slow Dissemination

The new Fender Stratocaster was by no means an overnight success, but then virtually nothing was in the musical instrument field in the 1950s. Back in the day, the word on potential new sensations—however truly sensational—disseminated far more slowly than we've become used to in the twenty-first century. Even a revolutionary new design's attainment of "classic" status was more a steady crawl than a breakneck sprint. Regardless, the Stratocaster seemed to have become more immediately and consistently recognized for the groundbreaking creation that it was than the Broadcaster had been four years before, and the "canoe paddle" and "plank guitar" quips from competitors in the guitar market were tellingly absent. As successful as the Broadcaster/Telecaster/Esquire design eventually proved to be, the Stratocaster was more obviously a work of considerable engineering and design prowess. As familiar as its many then-unique features are to us today, it's important to remember that there was nothing else even remotely like it in the guitar market of the 1950s.

Gifted to him by Leo Fender, R&B artist Pee Wee Crayton's Stratocaster might be the earliest one heard on record, having been played on Crayton's 1954 single "Do unto Others."

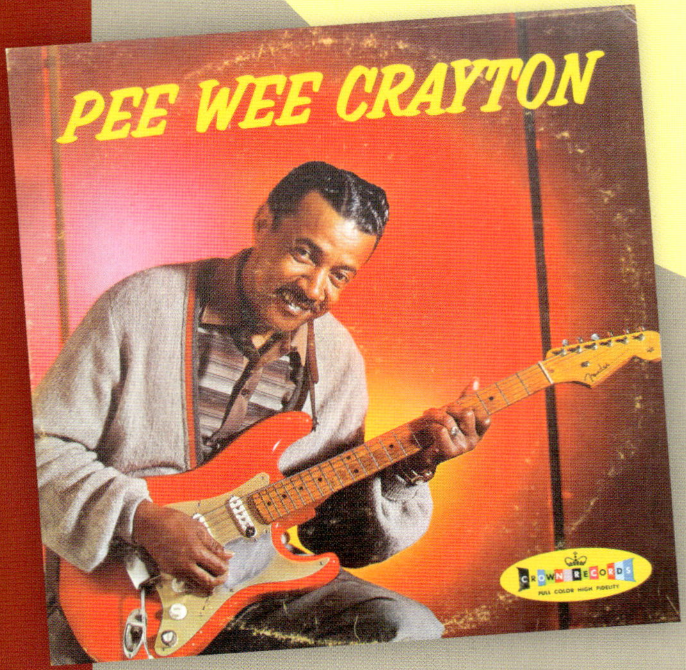

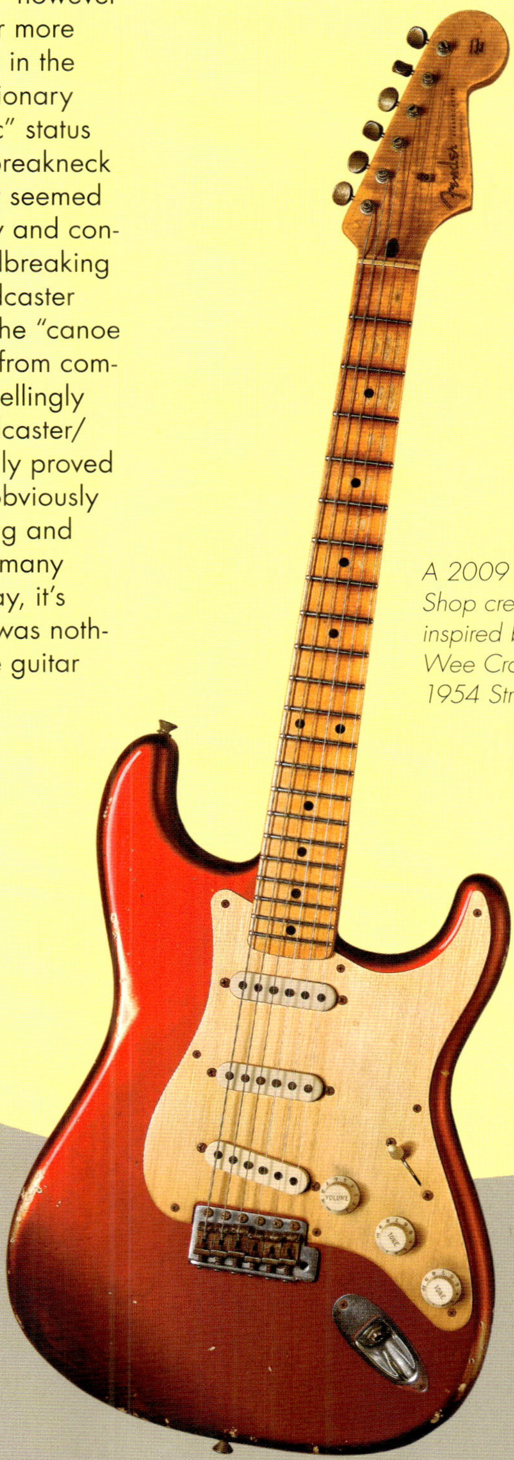

A 2009 Custom Shop creation inspired by Pee Wee Crayton's 1954 Stratocaster.

Early Adopters

For a guitar with such lithe, sultry, curvaceous lines that so boldly screamed "rock me!" from tip to tail, Leo Fender was never a big fan of the genre (still in its infancy), and initially the Stratocaster wasn't heavily promoted in that arena. As a result, this design that might otherwise have epitomized the revolutionary style and excitement of the new teen music sensation was surprisingly slow to work its way into the hearts and minds of the more radical players on that scene (though work its way it did). It's worth remembering that the Stratocaster was designed primarily for country and western players, and while we rarely associate the model with that genre today, these are the artists who first took it to prominence.

Bill Carson was clearly proud of his part in developing the Stratocaster and became one of its first prominent endorsers, although he was hardly a household name (in fact, this was an era when few guitar players could claim that status). Respect among your peers counted for something, though, and the early Stratocaster's uptake with professional musicians was as much a factor of the players' network and word of mouth as it was Don Randall's sales and promotion efforts. With few real guitar heroes at the time, and in lieu of a Les Paul (Gibson) or a Chet Atkins (soon representing Gretsch), Fender seemed happy enough to have a smiling, hatted-and-booted Carson cradling his Cimarron Red Strat in its trade-mag ads of the day.

THIS PAGE: *One of Bill Carson's later Stratocasters, a 1959 model in Fiesta Red finish.* OPPOSITE TOP: *Western swing guitarist Bill Carson became an early endorser of the Stratocaster and was proud of his role in the guitar's early development.* OPPOSITE BOTTOM: *Bill Carson's original Cimarron Red Stratocaster, which often appears black in monochrome photographs.*

The first artist to make use of the Stratocaster outside Fender's circle of test pilots was most likely Buddy Merrill, who was also very likely the first person to play a Stratocaster on TV. A young guitarist and steel guitarist from Torrey, Utah, Merrill was asked to join the Lawrence Welk Orchestra and perform on the nationally broadcast ABC-TV program in 1955 at only 18 years of age, after his mother submitted a disc recording of Merrill's playing to Welk's "All American" music contest. He brought his 1954 Stratocaster with him upon taking up the post—arguably a revolutionary instrument to apply to Welk's "champagne music," which generally appealed to an older crowd—and introduced the electric guitar to a generation of potential new Fender customers.

Having derided the Telecaster and brushed off Fender's efforts to get him to play one just a few years before, Texas Playboys guitarist Eldon Shamblin enthusiastically embraced a Stratocaster custom-finished in gold. One artist who *had* accepted the Broadcaster/Telecaster but was quick to step up to the Stratocaster when it arrived was Herschel "Speedy" Haworth. Less known today but a notable player of the era, Haworth was a sideman with Red Foley and Porter Wagoner, as well as the house guitarist and a regular cast member of the TV show *Ozark Jubilee* from 1955 to 1960, which frequently featured him riffing fleet-fingered instrumentals on his Strat and making emotive use of its new vibrato bridge in the process.

ABOVE: *Notable Stratocaster players of the pre-rock era were a world away from what was to come in a few short years. Take, for example, Buddy Merrill. The guitarist joined the Lawrence Welk Orchestra at just eighteen.* **OPPOSITE TOP:** *An unknown Fender employee (left) puts the finishing touches on a custom gold-finished 1954 Stratocaster for Texas Playboys guitarist Eldon Shamblin (far right) as Fender's Forrest White looks on beside him.* **OPPOSITE BOTTOM:** *Shamblin's well-worn gold Stratocaster after many years of playing.*

Similarly, the unique stylist Thumbs Carllile—a virtuosic player who held his guitar across his lap, lap-steel style, but fretted it with his fingers rather than using a slide—was a busy Strat-playing sideman and solo artist making regular appearances on *Ozark Jubilee*, and he was featured in Fender's promotional literature (albeit often misspelled as "Carlyle") as early as 1955.

One of the earliest guitarists to port the Stratocaster out of the country market was R&B and blues artist Pee Wee Crayton, whose early example with an anodized aluminum pickguard was custom finished in red (possibly the same hue that would later be known as Fiesta Red or Dakota Red). Gifted to Crayton by Leo Fender alongside a '54 Twin amp, this might also be the earliest Stratocaster heard on record, having been played on Crayton's 1954 single "Do Unto Others" (with a guitar introduction that sounds remarkably like that of the Beatles' "Revolution," recorded some fourteen years later).

Blues great Buddy Guy further helped establish the Stratocaster's prominence in that genre, taking up what was most likely a 1958 example after his early Les Paul goldtop was stolen. An even earlier proponent in the blues and R&B arenas, and one whose music in general had a significant influence on rock 'n' roll, was Ike Turner. Turner is believed to have taken up the Strat right from its arrival in 1954, and his occasionally extreme use of its vibrato bridge showed what an expressive piece of hardware it could be at a time when others were using it largely for subtle warbles and faux pedal-steel effects.

ABOVE LEFT: *Blues great Buddy Guy helped establish the Stratocaster's prominence in that genre.* ABOVE RIGHT: *Ike Turner is believed to have taken up the Stratocaster right from its arrival in 1954. He and partner Tina Turner are pictured here circa 1964.* OPPOSITE: *Prolific sideman and solo artist Thumbs Carllile appeared in Stratocaster promotional literature as early as 1955.*

THIS PAGE: *In the nascent realm of rock 'n' roll, Buddy Holly was an early devotee of the Stratocaster.* OPPOSITE TOP: *A 1956 Blonde Stratocaster with hang tags and original case.* OPPOSITE BOTTOM: *Rockabilly Gene Vincent (center) and his Blue Caps guitarist Johnny Meeks (left) wield matching Blonde Stratocasters in this publicity still. Also featured are a Precision Bass and tweed Twin Amp.*

Arguably, the first genuine pop idol to take the sultry new Fender model to the nation was Buddy Holly, who went through four Stratocaster guitars in his short career between 1955 and his untimely death in 1959. His first, likely a 1954 model acquired in 1955, was stolen from a tour bus in Michigan, and his second, a new '57 Stratocaster, was stolen from the band's station wagon during a restaurant stop in Saint Louis in April 1958. But Holly's use of these, all in standard Sunburst finish, helped to establish the model nationwide through his many TV and concert appearances.

Johnny Meeks, one of two guitarists who replaced Cliff Gallup in Gene Vincent's band the Blue Caps, was another early proponent of the Stratocaster as a rock 'n' roll instrument. Fellow Gene Vincent guitarist Howard Reed also played a Strat by the time the Blue Caps received their Fender endorsement in 1957, making them one of the earliest prominent rock 'n' roll bands to do so.

The Stratocaster was definitively ahead of its time, and despite this list of influential artists, the full potential of the design wasn't widely revealed until a decade later, when trailblazing guitarists wrangled every iota of its potential to produce genre-melding music, creating soundscapes virtually unimaginable at the time of the model's introduction and using Fender's masterpiece to expand the boundaries of popular music itself.

THIS PAGE: *Hank Marvin's 1959 Stratocaster was an exotic piece of kit in the British Isles at the time. Marvin's influence on the British Invasion guitarists who followed cannot be overstated. He and his band The Shadows are seen performing for Princess Margaret (seated) in the early 1960s.* OPPOSITE AND NEXT SPREAD: *An extremely rare 1957 Stratocaster finished in Gold-Red Sparkle and with its original case.*

Altered Specs

Having birthed such a radical and successful design, it's interesting to consider that Fender wasn't afraid to alter and update the Stratocaster's specs throughout the early years of its run, and virtually forever after. Some more notable early changes, however, might be considered because the company had rushed to introduce the new guitar to the market, nailing down some essential elements such as the Synchronized Tremolo bridge fairly late in the process.

Changes during the first few years of the guitar's existence perhaps were made largely to improve a design which normally may have had a more extended period of prototyping.

So while the new Stratocaster outwardly appeared much the same throughout the 1950s, myriad little changes were imposed upon its materials and components. Some were merely cosmetic (though they also introduced improved roadworthiness, in many cases), while others directly altered the feel and sound of the guitar.

(CONTINUED ON PAGE 82)

Plastics

The materials used for the Stratocaster's knobs, switch tip, pickup covers, tremolo-cavity cover, and pickguard changed quite rapidly throughout the early months and years of its existence. The latter first took the form of a thin piece of gold-anodized aluminum, though various forms of plastics were standard once the guitar was in full production later in 1954.

The earliest Stratocaster guitars off the line in the spring of 1954 (which some refer to as "pre-production" examples, though they are clearly "post-prototype") had slightly smaller knobs than we've become used to, made from a pearloid-like white polystyrene plastic that was occasionally almost translucent. This was followed in the summer of '54 by a more opaque polystyrene plastic (often referred to as Bakelite, although it wasn't) for the knobs and pickup covers, and thin white ABS (acrylonitrile butadiene styrene) plastic for the pickguards and trem-cavity cover. Brittle by nature, and molded quite thinly on the pickup covers in particular, the polystyrene material suffered heavy wear and breakages, which is likely what inspired Fender to eventually find a new form of plastic for these parts. As a result, original Strats from this era often display chipped or cracked knobs and pickup covers so worn from pick contact that the pickups' black-fiber top bobbins show through at the edges. These early polystyrene parts also have a more rounded appearance at their edges, which was a result of their molding process and not simply due to play wear.

Around September 1954, Fender started using a larger mold for the knobs. They were still made from the opaque white polystyrene formulation but took the classic and slightly larger shape that we're familiar with today. Partway into 1957, Fender started using the more modern ABS for the knobs, pickup covers, and switch tip, although these weren't universally changed out all at once—some early '57 Strats might carry ABS pickup covers and polystyrene knobs, for example.

These plastics would take Fender right into the CBS years in the following decade, with the exception of one more change near the end of the 1950s. Partway through 1959, a three-ply celluloid pickguard was adopted for the Stratocaster and other models, although its coincidence with other changes makes it something we'll discuss in more detail alongside the features of the 1960s Stratocaster guitars in the following chapter.

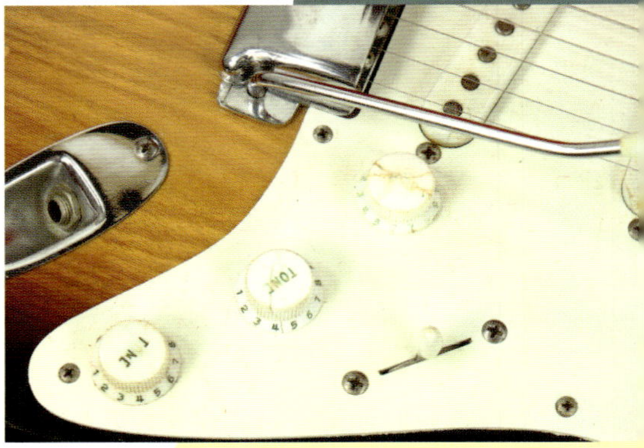

THIS PAGE: *Sturdier plastics used later—seen here on Blonde '55 and Blue Metallic '57 Stratocasters—helped reduce obvious wear.* OPPOSITE: *Early knobs and pickup covers were made of a brittle formulation that cracked easily with use, as seen on these 1954 and early-1955 Stratocasters*

Body Woods

As we have already seen, the first Stratocaster guitars off the bench were made with swamp ash, the wood Fender had settled on for the Telecaster after some early pine prototypes, and this remained the standard body wood until 1956. While the more highly figured ash was still used after for Strats given the Custom Color Blonde finish, alder became the standard wood beneath Sunburst and opaque Custom Color finishes.

The change was most likely a matter of availability and economy. Consistently lightweight and high-quality swamp ash had apparently become more difficult to find, and what could be sourced was arguably better used in the Telecaster, which came standard in Blonde; the Stratocaster's standard Sunburst finish with a dark edge hid much of the grain. The fact that alder is easier to carve and shape might also have influenced the shift.

The change in wood signaled a slight evolution in the Stratocaster's tone too: swamp ash promotes a somewhat more "scooped" voice in the Strat, with firm lows and clear highs but a somewhat recessed midrange. Alder, on the other hand, tends to enhance the guitar's midrange, giving it the impression of a somewhat thicker voice overall, while lows and highs appear a bit rounder. In any well-made guitar, these differences are often very subtle and are obviously compounded by many other components and build factors, but such contrasts do tend to define swamp ash Stratocaster guitars versus those made with alder.

A 1958 Stratocaster in three-tone Sunburst finish with alder body.

Neck Woods and Shapes

The Stratocaster was created with a one-piece maple neck with integral fretboard, which it retained until just before the turn of the decade. But the shape of that neck—something more felt in the hand than seen by the eye—changed steadily throughout the 1950s. The guitars from 1954 into early '55 had a chunky, rounded C shape, which segued into a beefy V (or "boat neck") profile in 1955. This V shape slimmed down slightly through 1956 and 1957 and then was rounded off into a slightly slimmer C shape for 1958, which became slimmer still in 1959 and 1960. Telecaster necks changed in much the same way through these years, and these neck profiles were rough-cut and finish-sanded by hand, therefore varying quite a bit depending on the worker who completed them. The changes from shape to shape rarely occurred overnight; often there's a transitional period between them that presents some hybrid or uncharacteristic profiles.

From around mid-1959, the Stratocaster's neck shape reflected a contemporary predilection for extremely thin necks, which were clearly considered "fast" at the time. About a year behind this trend, beginning partway into 1960, many Gibson electrics such as the Les Paul and SG were given similarly thin necks, which they retained for a few years before necks from both makers began to thicken up again. (Another significant change came to Fender necks in 1959, changing their look as much as their feel, but this is generally considered another key feature of the 1960s, so it will be addressed in the following chapter.)

Also worth noting here is that the headstocks of the first one hundred or so pre-production Stratocaster guitars display more rounded edges, which were hand-sanded to break the sharp angle of the saw cut and produce a softer radiused edge. All Stratocaster guitars after were shipped with more squared-off headstock edges, which were only lightly sanded to remove any genuine sharpness.

Electronics

As discussed in previous chapters, Fender had its blueprint for a pickup capable of producing the ideal sound from these guitars in place even before the official release of the Broadcaster/Esquire/Telecaster four years before. The Fender archetype—six Alnico rod magnets supported by vulcanized fiber top and bottom plates, with a narrow coil wound around them—was adapted to suit the Stratocaster. For the earliest Stratocaster pickups used on guitars through much of 1954, these rod-magnet polepieces were made from Alnico III, but Alnico V was generally used from 1955 onward. These early Alnico III poles were also a little wider in diameter than those that followed, at approximately 0.2" [5 mm] compared to 0.192" [4.9 mm] of a year or so later. Other than that, the standard specs of these pickups themselves didn't "officially" change much through the 1950s.

They did, however, vary quite a bit in their winding patterns and DC resistance readings (which merely represent the number of turns of 42 AWG wire wound around them) depending on who made them, how attentive to the task they were that day, and so forth. The trend in this variable is generally seen as a gradual increase in resistance as the decade progressed, with many very early Strat pickups showing readings in the mid-5k ohms range, while those nearer the end of the '50s can push toward 6k ohms.

Along with the increased coil windings came a slight enhancement of the Stratocaster's midrange response. But this sonic evolution roughly coincided with the move to alder as the standard body wood, which can also enhance midrange, so it's often difficult to pin down the difference in the respective sounds of, say, two original Stratocaster guitars from 1954 and 1957 without considering a range of factors (in fact, two vintage Strats off the bench on the same day in the same year can often sound quite different).

One notable change in the guitar's electronics was introduced very early in the run: the first one hundred or so pre-production Stratocaster guitars (those with the serial numbers stamped into the plastic tremolo cavity covers) were outfitted with 100k-ohm Volume and Tone potentiometers, while those after (with neck-plate serial numbers) carried 250k-ohm pots, the standard on Stratocaster guitars forever after. The lower-value pots of the early guitars can round off the treble response, somewhat taming the sharp highs otherwise produced by relatively low-wound pickups.

Finishes

Sunburst was the Stratocaster's standard finish from its time of release. This was first a one-color sunburst on the early pre-production guitars, which were sprayed at the body edges with a dark-brown color called Salem—which can sometimes almost appear black—that gave way to the natural ash color nearer the center. (Today the natural ash is usually seen tinted by the ageing of the nitrocellulose lacquer.) This was soon changed to a two-color 'burst, with the body first painted Canary Yellow then given a dark-brown-black Salem 'burst around the edges. In 1958 Fender expanded the Sunburst to a three-color finish, adding a red band between the edges and the center of the body, although this color has often faded on early three-tone Sunburst Stratocaster guitars, leaving them with an appearance similar to earlier two-tone guitars.

Blonde 1950s Stratocasters have often been dubbed "Mary Kaye Strats" because of their use in this iconic ad, although no guitar officially carried that designation in Fender sales sheets of the day.

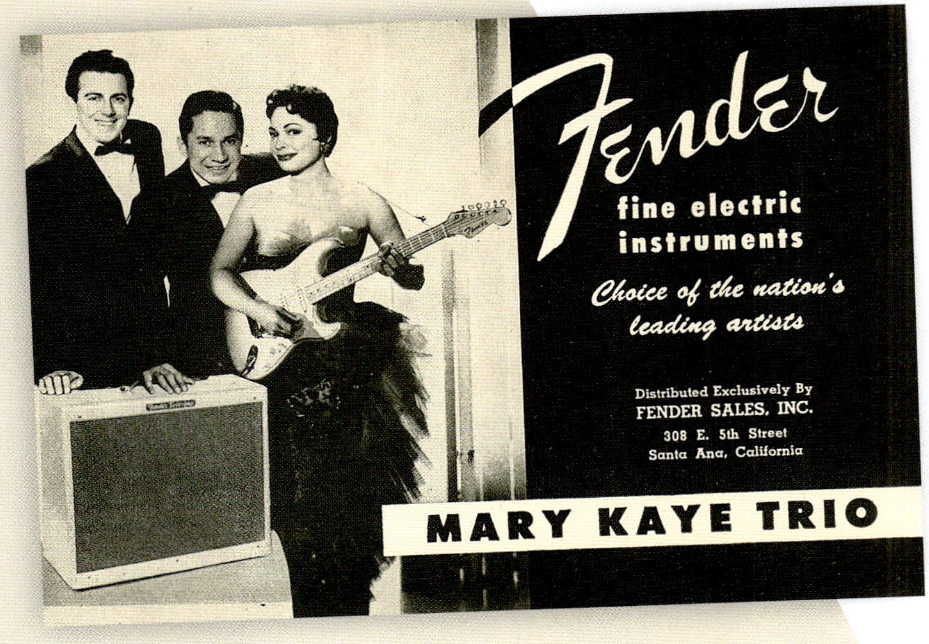

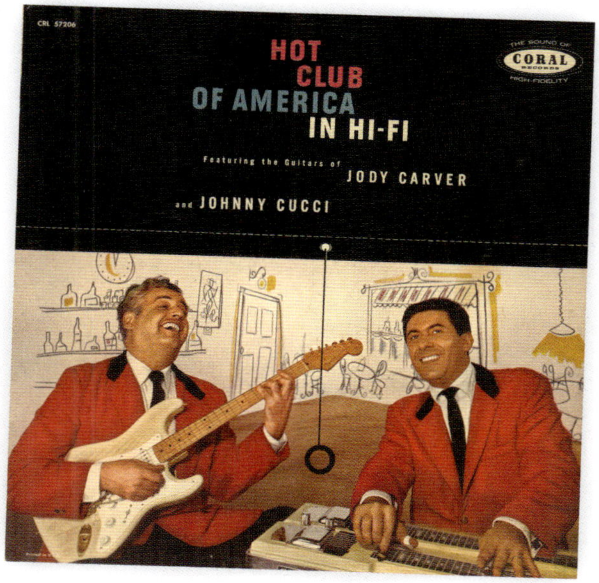

We already know of the red Stratocaster guitars made early on for Bill Carson and Pee Wee Crayton, and the gold one given to Eldon Shamblin, but prior to 1956, the application of anything other than Sunburst came as a one-off for a showpiece or artist guitar. The first official mention of the availability of any alternatives to the standard Sunburst Stratocaster came in a note at the bottom of a 1956 sales sheet, which read, "Stratocaster guitars are available in DuPont Duco colors of the player's choice at an additional 5% cost." Custom paint options had proved big sellers in the car industry in recent years, and it made sense to offer the same on electric guitars, especially as rock 'n' roll and the youth markets became bigger and bigger consumers of these solidbodies.

Although Blonde was standard for the Telecaster, it was considered a Custom Color for the Stratocaster and another of the earlier alternatives to Sunburst. One of the more famous early Custom Color Strats is referred to as the "Mary Kaye Stratocaster," actually finished in a translucent off-white 'burst that's slightly lighter than the Blonde Teles of the day, complemented by gold-plated hardware. The first of these was made in January 1956 and retained by Don Randall. Randall occasionally loaned it out for promotion or special occasions—including both a movie performance and a promotional photo with the Mary Kaye Trio around mid-1956—until it was given by him to Johnny Cucci after the guitarist had used the custom Strat for demos at the Fender booth throughout the 1956 summer NAMM show in New York City. In 1957 the trans-white Stratocaster with gold hardware was formally offered as a custom option in the catalog, although it was never officially listed as a "Mary Kaye" model.

A 1957 Stratocaster finished in Blue Metallic, before the Custom Colors were officially designated on any chart.

A Blonde 1955 Stratocaster with anodized pickguard.

Around this time, George Fullerton also gave the Custom Color notion a bump by pursuing several shades to try out on Fender guitars. As he put it, "One day, I went down to a local paint store and I started to explain to the man what I had in mind. I had him mix some paint there on the spot and finally we came up with a red color . . . Fiesta Red! I would say probably late 1957/early 1958. The Custom Colors came out about the time the Jazzmaster just came out. The reason I know that is because I had the color red put over one of the early manufactured Jazzmasters."[1]

For all this, Custom Color Stratocaster guitars from the 1950s are extremely rare and highly collectible as a result. Custom Colors became more prevalent in the 1960s alongside a more prominent and standardized exhibit of their availability in the Fender catalog, but Custom Color Stratocaster guitars would forever after be far pricier items on the vintage market than standard Sunburst Stratocaster guitars, which are still highly collectible.

Hardware

Alterations to the Stratocaster's hardware weren't particularly dramatic through the 1950s. Guitars made in the spring and early summer of '54 had round string holes punched in the trem-cavity covers on the back, and a look beneath these covers reveals relatively shallow holes in the steel inertia block, which anchors the strings' ball ends beneath the bridge. Guitars offered from the official release of the model in October 1954 had oval string holes in their back covers and slightly deeper holes in the bridge blocks, capable of retaining larger ball ends.

From 1954 the Strat's headstock was equipped with a round string tree to increase the break angle of the two highest-tuned strings from the nut to their tuner posts. Partway through 1956, this was changed to a thinner, bent-steel "butterfly" clip screwed flush to the face of the headstock. This type of string tree was slightly altered in 1959 with the addition of a metal spacer to lift the clip off the headstock, slightly decreasing the angle over the nut (a change likely made to improve tuning stability with vibrato use, since the strings are more likely to snag in the nut slots when a sharper angle is imposed at that point).

The Admen Cometh

Eleven years into the existence of the company, Fender stepped up to the big leagues in promotional terms. With two groundbreaking Spanish electric guitars in the market alongside several highly regarded amplifiers and steel guitars, Fender hired the Perine/Jacoby Agency of Newport Beach, California, in 1957 to embark on one of the most iconic campaigns ever launched by a musical-instrument company. Although it was a young agency, founded just one year before, Perine/Jacoby took the brief and ran with it. The resultant promotional campaign of more than a decade—referred to as the "You won't part with yours either" series, for the tagline attached to the elaborately staged and photographed ads—carried the style and heft of a much larger agency's work for a much larger company and has become part of the universal consciousness of vintage-guitar fans today.

Of his inspiration for the legendary ad series, Robert Perine later wrote, "I conceived the idea of doing a series of ads that would photographically show this relationship of guitar to player. Wouldn't it be interesting, I thought, to depict musicians of all ages unwilling to leave their wonderful, precious Fender guitars unattended. Why not play with this idea of attachment run amok, the needle hitting the peg on the possessiveness meter?"[2]

Over the years, following this theme, the Perine/Jacoby print ads showed Fender guitars strapped to the backs of jet pilots, scuba divers, downhill skiers, tank commanders, football players, motorcyclists, and parachutists; in the hands of skateboarders, mid-curl surfers, subway passengers, and country pickers on foot amid city traffic (the latter two apparently gig-bound, each with a tweed amp also in hand); and perched on their own in a wide assortment of unlikely settings—though invariably with a youthful slant or an exciting or romantic activity going on as backdrop. On occasion, later in the 1960s, Perine even featured his own daughter in some of the catalog shots, noting a particular favorite in 1968 that showed her climbing into his own red Thunderbird with a red Fender Coronado in hand.

LEFT: *Robert Perine captured this image of the Fender shipping dock and what looks to be rather recently painted signage.* OPPOSITE AND FOLLOWING SPREAD: *Examples from the iconic "You won't part with yours either" ad series devised by Robert Perine and Ned Jacoby.*

You won't part with yours either*
Where musicians go, you'll find Fender!
*To help you select the finest instrument available for the young student your leading music dealer has a complete line of Fender Fine Electric Instruments (like the three-quarter size "Musicmaster" guitar and Harvard Amp shown above).
Fender SALES INC.
308 EAST FIFTH ST. • SANTA ANA, CALIF.

You won't part with yours either*
ELECTRICAL ACCESS
NO STEP
JET
INTAKE
Where musicians go, you'll find Fender!
*For your personal selection see the complete line of Fender fine electric instruments (like the famous "Stratocaster" guitar shown above) on display at leading music dealers throughout the world.
Fender SALES INC.
308 EAST FIFTH ST. • SANTA ANA, CALIF.

ARMY TIMES
July, 1966

Chapter 5

SWINGING INTO THE '60s

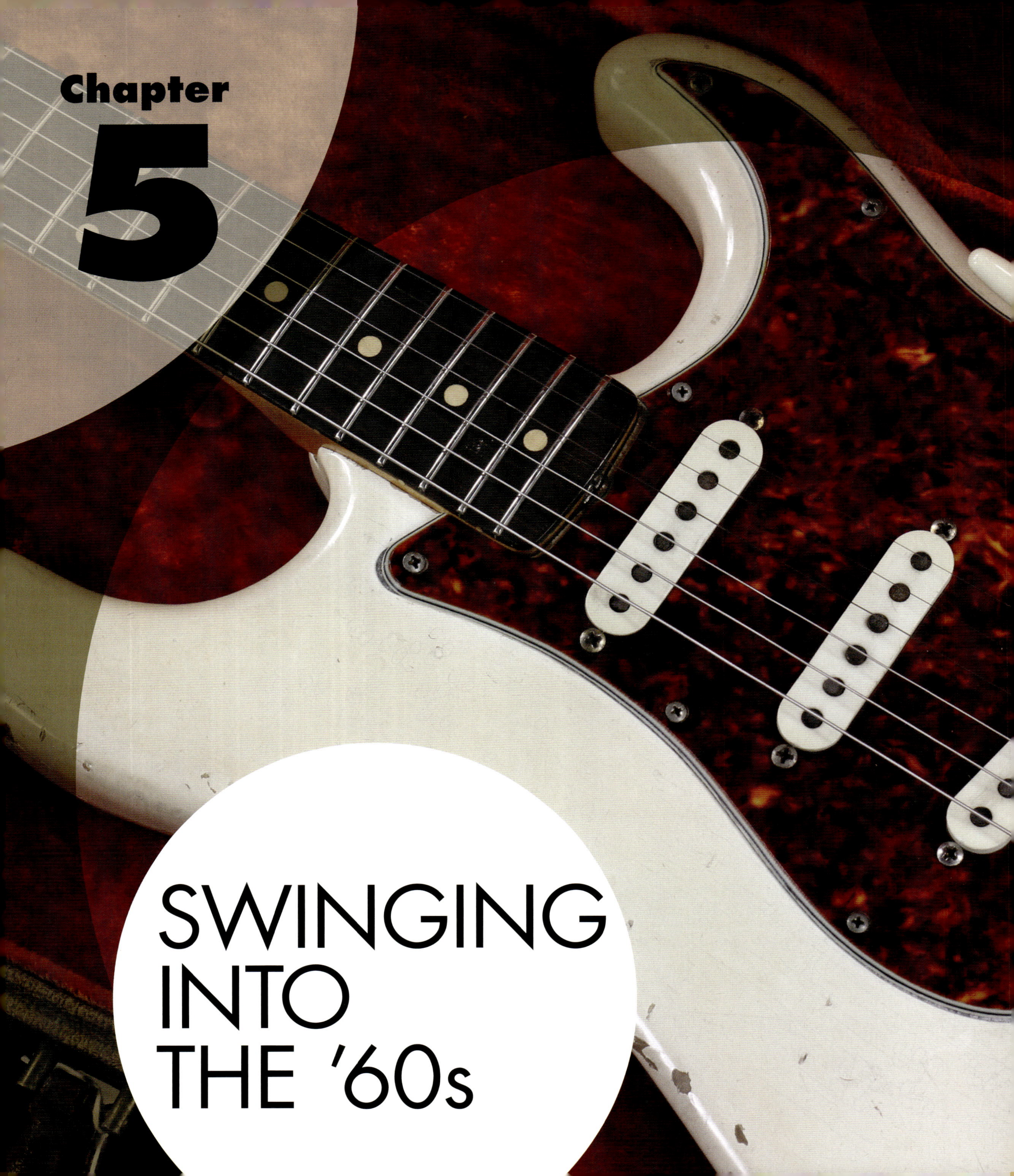

A Move Toward Modernization

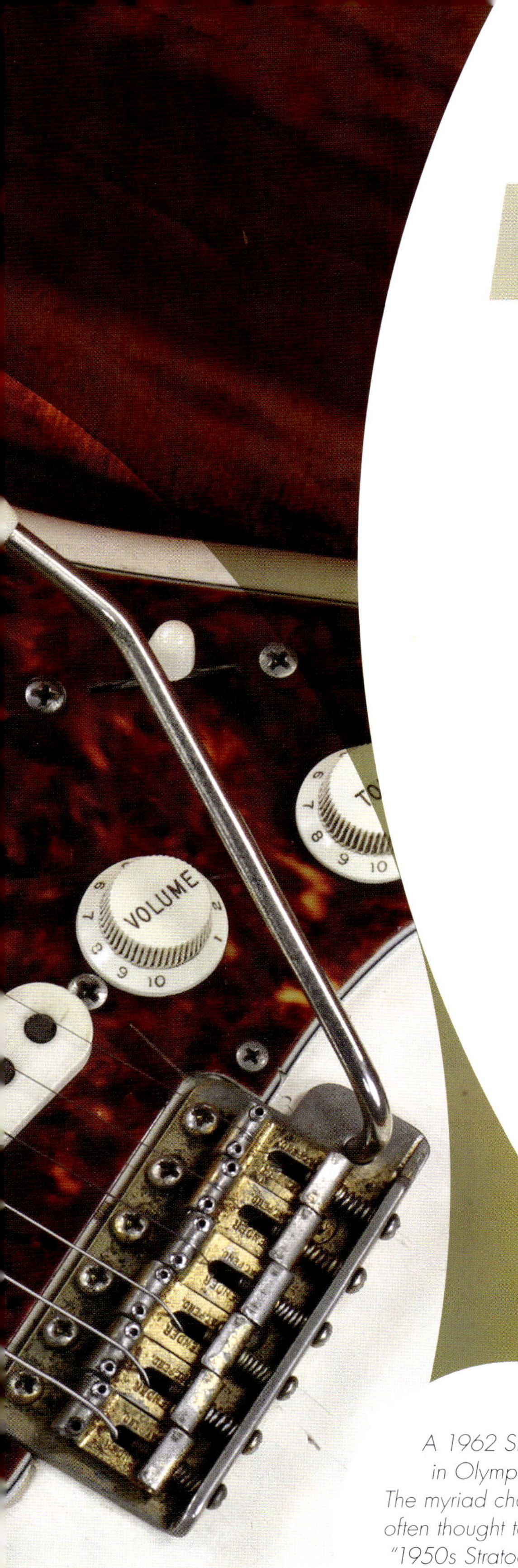

A 1962 Stratocaster in Olympic White. The myriad changes that are often thought to distinguish a "1950s Stratocaster" from a "1960s Stratocaster" were actually implemented over time.

While Stratocaster guitars produced the first decade or so of the model's existence all fall under the highly desirable "pre-CBS" banner, most players and collectors perceive significant differences in specifications and appearance depending on whether a specific guitar originates from the '50s or early '60s. In truth, the Stratocaster, like most significant Fender guitars, evolved gradually from one state to the other, absorbing myriad changes imposed upon it year to year. But larger bundles of alterations tend to come together to define "a '50s Strat" versus "a '60s Strat," even though there can be significant variations beneath those two umbrellas.

Many of the changes to specifications that we now use to identify Stratocaster guitars of the 1960s actually were enacted upon the model just before the turn of the decade, and some of the most significant were introduced across Fender's entire range. In fact, the chronological corner turned from 1959 to 1960 encompassed dramatic updates throughout the company's catalog—developments that comprised a thorough modernization of Fender products.

Arguably even more noticeable than the changes to the guitars were those to the amplifier range. Beginning in late 1959 and consolidated across most of the amp lineup by the end of 1960, Fender reconfigured most of its amps from the upper-rear-mounted chassis and control panel of the tweed-era amps to the front-mounted panel used thereafter. It was a revolutionary refresh of the industry standard and represented a demarcation point between the outdated and the modern. Covering these amps in Tolex, a textured fabric-backed vinyl, emphasized the turning point further. (Other than the occasional odd duck, only the humble Champ retained its tweed-era cabinet after 1960, and that was more and more often also covered in Tolex before the combo was completely redesigned in 1964.)

THIS PAGE AND OPPOSITE: *A range of '60s Stratocasters displays the diversity of the model's look from the early to mid- to late parts of the decade.*

The first Fender amplifier to be covered in Tolex (light brown, in this case) was the new Vibrasonic that debuted at the summer NAMM show of 1959. A sales sheet penned at that time declared,

The Fender Vibrasonic Amplifier is one of the finest musical instrument amplifiers ever offered to the buying public. It offers the musician tremendous distortion-free power, plus one of the most advanced circuits in the amplifier field. . . . The over-all appearance of the Fender Vibrasonic Amp is sleek and modern in every respect and is enhanced by the rich textured vinyl fabric covering.

Rather boastful claims, perhaps, but entirely accurate. In addition to the ultramodern look, the new lineup of Fender amps that followed the Vibrasonic's lead were packed with revamped circuits intended to enhance the power and clarity that Fender deemed essential for professional guitarists to cut through the mix on stage. As such, during the early 1960s they ushered in an entirely new breed of "Fender sound," albeit one recognizable as an extension of the characteristics already sought from the company's guitars.

Rose Parade

The biggest distinguishing change to hit the Stratocaster itself was one that had been introduced during the development of the Jazzmaster guitar in 1957 and unveiled to the public when that new model hit the streets in 1958. As part of its effort to create a guitar for the jazz player—assumed to be more staid in his or her tastes—Fender complemented the Jazzmaster's Sunburst finish with a rosewood fingerboard atop the maple neck. The feature essentially failed its stated mission in that regard, given that few jazz players ever accepted the model that had been named for them. But the company applied the rosewood fingerboard to both the Stratocaster and Telecaster midway through 1959, and the dark slice of South American timber became one of the defining characteristics of the early 1960s Fender guitars.

Although the addition of a rosewood fingerboard to a guitar intended to appeal to more traditional players makes total sense, it has often been said (and both motivations could indeed be true) that sometime around 1957, Leo Fender saw one of his existing guitars with an all-maple neck on television and was dismayed to see the dark smudged patches where the finish had worn away from the otherwise light-colored natural maple fingerboard. The move to rosewood certainly provided a means to eliminating that grimy-looking wear.

Reports also indicate that Fender sales reps had been fielding dealer inquiries about the availability of a rosewood fingerboard on the Telecaster and Stratocaster for quite some time. Not only would the darker fingerboard cure the issue of dirty-looking finger-wear patches on the board, but it would also bring Fender's guitars in line with more established instruments and perhaps help them appeal to players still hesitant to accept these "plank" guitars—which kind of takes the issue full circle behind the use of this wood on the Jazzmaster.

Most players knew that the addition of a rosewood fingerboard to an otherwise all-maple neck didn't merely change the looks, but it also brought some tonal adjustments to the formula. The sonic alteration is usually heard as a little more warmth, roundness, and smoothness, with a tad less of the sparkle, bite, and immediacy of the all-maple neck with integral fingerboard. These are fine points, though, and myriad other factors in the construction and components of

any individual Stratocaster can make it difficult to discern this shift with any great accuracy.

"Using different materials for the rosewood," says former Fender master builder Chris Fleming, "Indian rosewood as opposed to Brazilian rosewood—or what we use a lot of now, which is Madagascan rosewood—makes a lot of difference in itself. My favorite rosewood to use on a Fender is Indian. Most [rosewood used by Fender] was Brazilian up until the early '60s, and then it switched to mostly Indian because in the mid-1960s Brazilian began becoming a problem. But Brazilian, in my opinion, is a bit too bright. Once again, though, it depends on the actual piece. Brazilian can be very dense and ringing, which is nice in some combinations . . . but I'm not wild about Brazilian on maple, although other guys will tell you I'm crazy."[1]

ABOVE: *Luther Perkins, guitarist in Johnny Cash's Tennessee Two, joins Leo Fender to test out the new Jazzmaster through a prototype for the also-new Vibrolux amplifier.* **LEFT:** *The Jazzmaster provided a vehicle for Fender's use of the rosewood fingerboard before the feature hit the entire guitar range.* **OPPOSITE:** *For several years from mid-1959 the rosewood fingerboard was standard on the Stratocaster, as seen here on a Foam Green 1959 model.*

The rosewood fingerboards first applied to Stratocaster necks in 1959 were sawn with a flat underside and glued to a flat neck face, a style that has since been dubbed the "slab board" for its thick, flat-bottomed appearance. Midway through 1962, Fender began radiusing the top face of the maple neck and the underside of the fingerboard, which enabled the use of a slightly thinner piece of rosewood. The fingerboards created using this method came to be known as "laminated" or "round-lam" fingerboards. (By special request from the mid-1960s, and as an official option from 1967, maple fingerboards would again be available. Until 1969, such necks were made much like the slab rosewood fingerboards, with a separately milled piece of maple glued to the face of the neck, a construction now known as a "maple cap" neck.)

Many players have expressed a preference for the earlier slab board necks, usually in the belief that the thicker piece of rosewood is somehow superior. Fleming's thoughts on the matter, however, somewhat dispel this perception:

Somebody asked me why I thought Leo decided to do round lams, and although I can't know for sure, I think it was for a couple of reasons. One is that he liked the idea of the maple being more of a majority of the wood, and he liked the idea that it was kind of a custom way to do it, it was proprietary. And I'd also like to think that he liked the sound of it. I feel like the slab 'board was the way that they did it because they had to figure out how to do it quickly. Then they had to tool up to make the rounded 'board and never turned back.

Considered in this light, it's clear that the thinner, rounded rosewood board used after mid-1962 took more work to produce, and the earlier flat-bottomed board never encompassed so thick a piece of rosewood to make it significantly costlier from a supply perspective than the thinner board. In any case, Fleming, for one, declares the tonal difference between the two to be negligible, if detectible at all.

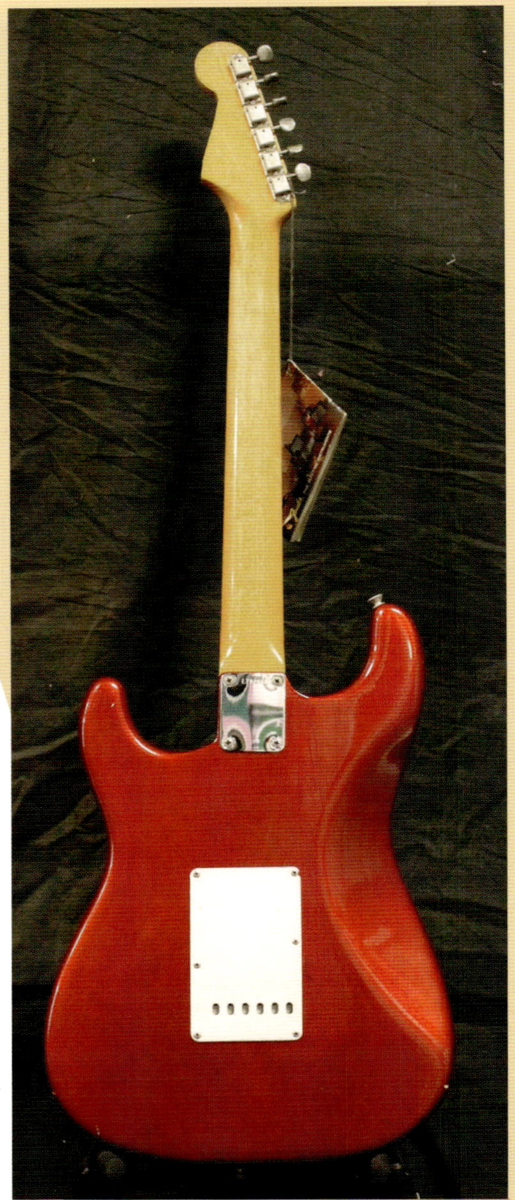

The maple fingerboard was a popular option again from 1965 onward, albeit achieved with a separate piece of maple (a "cap") attached to the neck after the truss rod was installed (note the lack of "skunk stripe" on the back of the neck of this small-headstock '65 Strat).

Thinning Necks

A perceived preference for thinner necks in much of the industry for a few years at the turn of the decade also took hold at Fender, leading to carving the necks with far less depth behind the lower frets. The "shapes per era" of vintage Fender necks has never been easy to catalog because these parts were always final-sanded by hand to something within a general agreed tolerance, a process that allowed for several variables and resulted in a relatively wide range of shapes and sizes.

A neck's "depth" refers to the thickness of the wood as measured with calipers from the center point of the fingerboard just behind the fret to the center of the back of the neck, usually taken just behind the first and the twelfth frets. Broadly speaking, Stratocaster necks of the 1950s fell in the 0.85" [2.2 cm] range, give or take a few hundredths of an inch. Some were a little slimmer and some as thick as 0.90" [2.3 cm] or more, with the occasional beefy example topping out above that.

As the end of the decade approached, these depths tended to measure somewhat shallower and became significantly shallower still in 1960–1963 or so. Many Stratocaster guitars from the early '60s have depth measurements of slightly less than 0.80" [2.03 cm] behind the first fret, with 0.79" [2 cm] and 0.78" [1.98 cm] being particularly common. Just before the end of the '50s, the shape (a.k.a. "profile") of most Stratocaster necks had rounded out into a C from the soft V shape characteristic of guitars from 1957.

This basic shape was retained, broadly speaking, as the new decade dawned, although the slimming down of the necks also put that rounded C on something of a diet, some tending toward what is described as an "oval" profile. Nevertheless, the common Fender neck profiles of the early '60s are generally considered by most players to be very comfortable, at least if they're not entirely too thin for an individual's hand in the first place, and many that start off very slim grow to a more hand-filling carve as you slide up the neck.

Rolling on into 1964 and 1965, the Stratocaster's neck still generally sported a rounded C or oval shape, but it also started to thicken up again, often leaning into the low- or even mid-0.80" [2.03 cm] range. In addition to being primary characteristics of Stratocaster guitars from different periods within the full range of the pre-CBS era, these ever-changing neck shapes and depths have given today's Fender, and the Custom Shop in particular, some period-correct specifications to nail down the accuracy of reissue guitars manufactured several decades after the originals.

A craftsman works on a stack of rosewood fingerboard necks in the Fender facilities in the early 1960s.

Pickup Components

Following the move away from the 0.20"-diameter [5 mm] pole pieces in the earliest '54 Strats to the 0.192" [4.9 mm] diameter thereafter, Stratocaster pickups didn't change dramatically for several years, other than varying according to the specs imposed on them by the wide tolerances involved in the winding process. The trend in this department was toward winding somewhat greater lengths of wire onto the coils as the 1950s progressed into the 1960s, meaning the average DC resistance readings in the mid-5k-ohms range of the mid-'50s moved well into the lower 6k-ohms range by the early '60s. (For some reason, many Strats from 1959 show an exception to this rule, with pickups that are a little "cooler" than those immediately before and after.)

The next significant component change came with another move to the use of even smaller-diameter polepieces partway through 1963, made from Alnico V rods with a diameter of 0.187" [4.7 mm]. It was a minor change, certainly, but one that is sometimes thought to have focused the pickup's magnetic field a little more tightly, leading to even brighter and clearer tones.

Arguably more significant than that, in 1964, Fender switched from heavy formvar-coated 42 AWG coil wire to plain enamel-coated 42 AWG wire. Although the wire itself was nominally the same, the insulation that protected it from shorting out when wound tightly into a coil was now of a thinner, more modern variety. This meant the same length of wire wound onto a Stratocaster pickup resulted in a more compact coil overall, giving the pickup itself a sharper focus and a tighter, brighter tone.

Fender's tendency to wind hotter and hotter Strat pickups through the 1950s and into the early to mid-1960s was somewhat reversed from the mid-1960s onward. Through the latter part of that decade and into the early 1970s, Fender's pickup winders packed less of the plain-enamel wire onto their coils, generally decreasing their output as a result (these can still vary within any period, occasionally dramatically).

Approximately coinciding with the change to plain-enamel-coated wire in 1964 (though not necessarily precisely so), Fender also started using light-gray fiber (Forbon) bottom plates on its pickups. This material has no effect on the sound of the pickups in and of itself but is generally seen as one of the more obvious indicators of pickups made from the mid- to late-1960s (some guitarists have claimed instances of finding gray-bottom Stratocaster guitars wound with earlier formvar wire, so apparently there was a crossover period, as with so many Fender specifications). The gray-bottom material got a little darker still at some point in the early 1970s.

Classy Plastics

Through 1959, Fender also began changing both the material used for the Stratocaster's pickguard and the way it was attached. By the time the change was complete, the single-ply white plastic pickguard attached with eight screws—one of the identifying characteristics of Strats of the '50s—was replaced by a three-ply celluloid pickguard held on with eleven screws. On the way from the former to the latter, Fender transitioned through a mix-and-match variety of configurations, including single-ply guards held in place with more screws and three-ply attached with fewer than would be normal. In 1959 Fender also began using multi-ply faux-tortoiseshell pickguards on several guitars. These are fairly rare on the Stratocaster but are most likely to be found on early to mid-'60s examples finished in Olympic White or occasionally in Sunburst.

The three-ply celluloid guards that eventually became one of the denominators of the early to mid-'60s Stratocaster guitars was ostensibly a white-black-white configuration, although the outside of its top layer displayed a very slightly greenish hue, one that often took on a more minty-green appearance with age. These pickguards also shrunk with age, a condition that can cause cracking near the screws holes or difficulty with remounting after removal for maintenance. On top of all that, the celluloid could be unstable to work with and was highly flammable.

OPPOSITE: *Winding pickups at the Fender factory in 1966.*

The three-ply pickguard further dressed up the Stratocaster at the turn of the decade. Early examples tended to shrink and crack, as on this 1964 Daphne Blue Stratocaster. The plastic used for the pickguard on the 1965 Sherwood Green Metallic example proved more durable.

Around late 1964 going into 1965, Fender changed the pickguard material once again to a more stable three-ply white-black-white plastic. At a glance, these pickguards often look very similar to the preceding celluloid guards, but while they can yellow somewhat with age and UV exposure, they were originally more a proper white than the "very, very light green" of the celluloid guards and also didn't tend to shrink as much.

Regardless of the material used, with their three-ply construction and the "multi-ply" look revealed by the pickguard's beveled edge, both types of '60s pickguards lent the Stratocaster a slightly classier aesthetic and one better allied to more traditional-looking electric guitars. And although this was a stock look on standard Sunburst examples, it arguably enhanced the growing number of Custom Color Stratocaster guitars even more.

Custom Colors Consolidated

Fender semiofficially—and rather casually—offered up the concept of Custom Color finishes as early as 1956, and of course some special-order and artist guitars were given nonstandard finishes right from the start. Even so, examples of Custom Color Stratocaster guitars from the 1950s are extremely rare. While not plentiful in the 1960s by any means, and certainly still rare enough to be highly desirable and very collectible, more and more nonstandard finishes came out of Fullerton at the turn of the decade.

Fender's more formal standardization and proliferation of the Custom Color process clearly played a part in this, but the evolving culture of the day likely had a hand in it too. The electric guitar was becoming one of the totems of youth culture and central to popular music in general, while the styles of the times tipped further toward the colorful and flamboyant.

Fender published its first formal Custom Color chart in 1960. It included fourteen official paint options plus Blonde, each of which could be ordered through a Fender dealer at a 5 percent premium on the guitar's list price. If you were a buyer of the day with an eye to the future—several decades into the future—it was money well spent, considering the price these guitars fetch today. Compared to guitars from the same year and similar condition, a Custom Color on a pre-CBS Stratocaster will today add far more than 5 percent to its value, often something in the 25 to 30 percent range, or even as much as a 50 percent premium for the particularly rare colors.

Colors on the official 1960 Custom Finishes chart included the following:

- Lake Placid Blue Metallic
- Daphne Blue
- Sonic Blue
- Shoreline Gold Metallic
- Olympic White
- Burgundy Mist Metallic
- Black
- Sherwood Green Metallic
- Inca Silver Metallic
- Foam Green
- Surf Green
- Fiesta Red
- Dakota Red
- Shell Pink

An additional option not listed on the chart but mentioned in its caption was the Tele-like Blonde finish, which was almost invariably applied over an ash body. In 1963, Shell Pink was dropped and Candy Apple Red Metallic was added. Two years later, in 1965, Daphne Blue, Shoreline Gold Metallic, Burgundy Mist Metallic, Sherwood Green Metallic, Surf Green, and Inca Silver Metallic were also dropped, replaced by Blue Ice Metallic, Firemist Gold Metallic, Charcoal Frost Metallic, Ocean Turquoise Metallic, Teal Green Metallic, and Firemist Silver Metallic.

(CONTINUED ON PAGE 112)

Sunburst
LAKE PLACID BLUE METALLIC
LUCITE 2876-L
DAPHNE BLUE
DUCO 2804
SONIC BLUE
DUCO 2295
SHORELINE GOLD METALLIC
LUCITE 2935-L
OLYMPIC WHITE
LUCITE 2818-L

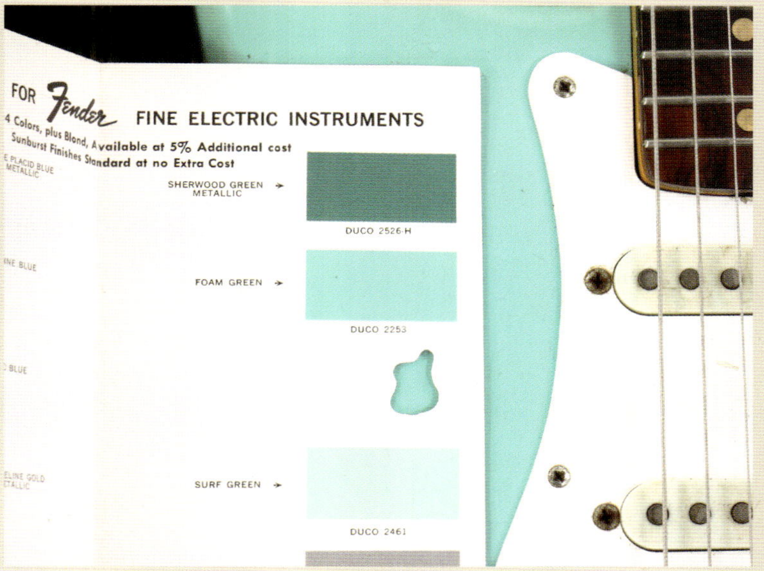

THIS SPREAD AND NEXT: *The Custom Color feature gained in popularity in the early '60s, as displayed by these Stratocasters from 1959 to 1964, several shown with their matching color charts.*

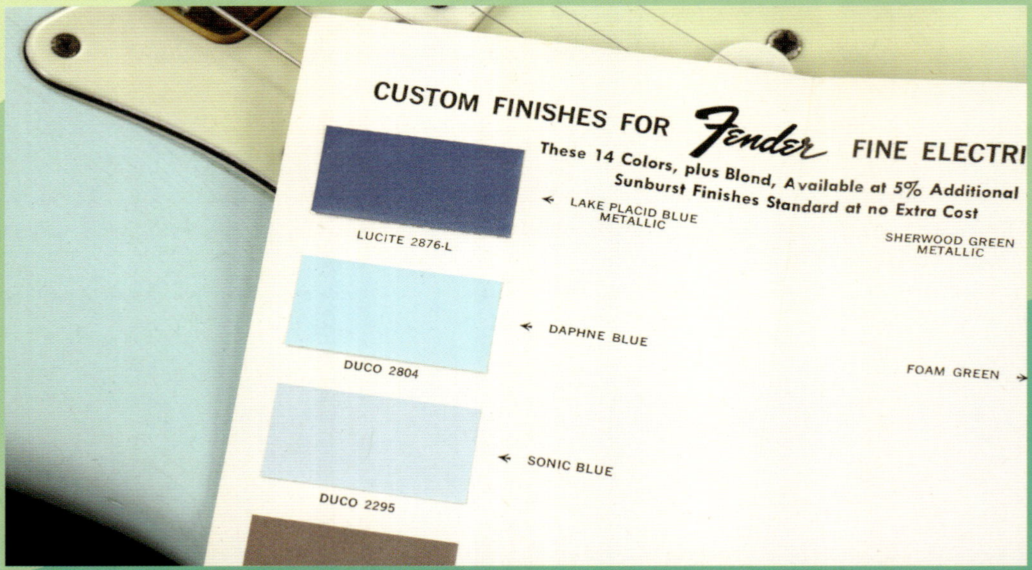
CUSTOM FINISHES FOR Fender FINE ELECTRI
These 14 Colors, plus Blond, Available at 5% Additional
Sunburst Finishes Standard at no Extra Cost
LAKE PLACID BLUE METALLIC
LUCITE 2876-L
SHERWOOD GREEN METALLIC
DAPHNE BLUE
DUCO 2804
FOAM GREEN
SONIC BLUE
DUCO 2295

Fender
STRATOCASTER

BLUE ICE METALLIC
4692-L
SONIC BLUE
2295
FIREMIST GOLD METALLIC
4579-LH
CHARCOAL FROST METALLIC
4618-L

Spraying Stratocaster bodies in the paint booth in 1963.

In what seemed quite a natural rock 'n' roll tie-in, most of these colors matched paints used by one or another Detroit automaker from the late 1950s to the mid-1960s, and Fender's custom-colored guitars could see their twins in cars made by Pontiac, Chevrolet, Ford, Cadillac, Lincoln, Buick, Mercury, Oldsmobile, and DeSoto.

Most Custom Colors were ordered via local dealers, so guitars weren't always built from the ground up with that particular option in mind. As a result, unbeknownst to their new owners, many were finished in the standard Sunburst before being shot with a Custom Color and sent on their way. Over time, playing wear imposed on some Custom Color Strats occasionally reveals a fresh undercoat of vibrant Sunburst, even if the guitar was officially a Custom Color from the factory.

Meanwhile, Fender's effort to liven up the standard Sunburst finish with a central band of red, begun mid-1959, took hold in the early '60s thanks to a refinement in the process. The standard finishing procedure was to spray the sanded body in a clear primer coat to seal and fill the grain (done using a product called Fullerplast from 1963 onward), dip it in a vat of yellow stain, and then spray the edges in black lacquer to create the original two-tone Sunburst look before hitting it with a clear coat of lacquer.

After the aniline red band on three-tone Sunburst guitars of 1959 and early 1960 was found to fade, making them appear much like two-tone 'bursts from previous years, Fender changed to a red that better withstood exposure and the rigors of time. The result was a more prominent three-tone Sunburst that retained a vibrant red in its center band—sometimes so vibrant that the slightly gaudy results have been labeled "target 'bursts" or "bullseye 'bursts" by later players and collectors.

The Jaguar Roars

Come 1962 the Stratocaster found itself two notches down in the standings for priciest guitar in the Fender catalog. The pricepoint leader from 1954 to 1958, the Stratocaster was knocked into second place by the Jazzmaster that came out that year. Then in 1962, Fender released the fancy, feature-packed new Jaguar model with the highest list price in the lineup.

The arrangement sounds rather backward today when vintage Jaguars (though rising in price and desirability) generally command the lowest prices of Fender's four main professional-grade electric guitars, given instruments from the same year, of similar condition, and bearing standard finishes. Considering the effort that went into the Jaguar's construction, however, and the plethora of deluxe features it carried, the situation is understandable from the manufacturer's perspective in 1962.

The Jaguar was made to a shorter 24" [60.9 cm] scale length that nevertheless featured twenty-two frets rather than the twenty-one of the Tele and Strat, which Fender apparently believed might appeal to Gibson players and otherwise seemed to be aimed at the burgeoning surf and instrumental guitar scenes in general. It carried two single-coil pickups that were basically designed along the traditional Fender template—and not unlike Stratocaster pickups when their covers were removed—but had an additional U-shaped metal "claw" that both helped shield the coils from noise and focus their magnetic field above the poles.

In addition to the specs cited above and the usual Fender construction formula, the Jaguar had both lead and rhythm switching circuits like the Jazzmaster, with a more deluxe three-switch pickup selector system for the lead circuit that offered on/off for each pickup plus a mid-cut switch (a.k.a. "strangle" switch) that applied to both. Like the Jazzmaster, the rhythm circuit bypassed the lower-bout volume and tone controls and cut the bridge pickup out of the circuit. The Jaguar also carried the same relatively complex "floating tremolo" partnered with a rocking bridge that was introduced on the Jazzmaster, but with a switchable foam-padded mute that the Jazzmaster lacked (thought to be useful for that "ticky-ticky" palm-muted sound often heard in surf music, while eliminating the need for palm-muting itself).

Upon its first appearance in the Fender Price List of July 1962, the standard Jaguar in Sunburst finish listed at $379.50, with the Jazzmaster a full $30 cheaper, the Stratocaster in Sunburst with tremolo at $289.50, and the Telecaster in Blonde at $209.50. Although the Jaguar found favor with plenty of surf and pop guitarists through the mid-1960s, it never quite attained the flagship status Fender obviously intended for it. Shifting trends in popular music that were just a few years down the road, and the patronage of some of the biggest guitar stars yet, would put the Stratocaster firmly back front and center.

(CONTINUED ON PAGE 116)

Robert Perine's illustration for the cover of the 1964–1965 catalog displays Fender's diverse ambitions of the day.

THIS SPREAD: *Unveiled in 1962, the Jaguar knocked the Stratocaster to third place on Fender's price list. It never usurped the Stratocaster's flagship status, becoming most popular with surf bands of the day. Carl Wilson of the Beach Boys famously wielded one, while bandmate Al Jardine (center) mostly stuck with his Stratocaster.*

High-Volume Amplification

Also central to shifting trends in Fender's overall development in the early '60s was the quest for high-volume amplifiers to suit the larger and larger halls played by popular groups. The company released its first high-powered amplifier in 1958 by doubling the tweed Twin's output stage from two 5881 tubes to four. Developments through the course of 1959 that led to the start of the Tolex-covered line also saw R&D efforts focused on a new style of "piggyback" (a.k.a. stack) set with separate amplifier head and extension speaker cabinet, pointing toward the ideal format for delivering increased power to the people.

Fender's 80-watt Showman hit the stage in 1960 in this new piggyback format, but R&D for the model was still highly active through the next couple of years. Stratocaster-playing surf guitarist Dick Dale made the case for increased power more strongly than perhaps anyone else at the time through his struggles to be heard over crowds of two to three thousand surfer-stomping teens at the Rendezvous Ballroom in Balboa, California, nearly every weekend of the year.

LEFT: *The 2004 Dick Dale Signature Chartreuse Sparkle Stratocaster.* OPPOSITE: *In addition to slinging a Stratocaster, surf rocker Dale was a driving force in Fender's development of more powerful amplifiers.*

After giving Leo Fender an earful about his struggles with failing amps and inadequate volume levels, so the story goes, Dale was conscripted as a test pilot to bludgeon new evolutions of the Showman into submission until he and Fender landed on a design that could take the punishment. Advances such as the use of a bigger output transformer and high-powered JBL 12" [30 cm] and 15" [38 cm] speakers finally got the job done. By 1962 the 100-watt Dual Showman with 2x15" [2x38 cm] cabinet arguably represented the most powerful guitar amplifier on earth. Come the mid- to late-'60s, an entirely new breed of hard-rocking guitarists from both sides of the Atlantic would show the world what a Stratocaster could do through raging high-powered "full-stack" rigs.

LEFT: *Bob Dylan in the studio with a Stratocaster in early 1965. Later that year he infamously "went electric" at the Newport Folk Festival on a three-tone Sunburst.* OPPOSITE: *A 1965 three-tone Sunburst Stratocaster with Band-Master amp and original shipping cartons.*

SERIAL NO.
MODEL
STANDARD GUITAR
HANDLE WITH CARE
CALIFORNIA
Fender
FINE ELECTRIC INSTRUMENTS
CAUTION
DO NOT DROP
SERIAL NO
Band-Master
NORMAL
VIBRATO
TOLEX
Fender

Chapter

6

A TIME OF CHANGE

CBS Takes the Helm

At the dawn of 1964, Fender employed approximately five hundred workers in a factory complex that spanned twenty-seven buildings across its large campus in Fullerton, California. Sales were riding high in a booming industry, and Fender's brand recognition was at its peak—so why sell out to a corporate overlord? That's a question long pondered by fans of vintage Fender guitars and guitar-history aficionados alike. And it isn't tied up into any one neat bow of an answer.

The forces pushing toward Fender's sale to Columbia Broadcasting System (CBS) really encompassed at least three main converging factors, none of which had anything to do with a downturn in business or managerial struggles that often lead to the sale of a company. In simple terms, these include the confluence of Leo Fender's ongoing health struggles (or at least his own perceptions of such), his desire to land a payout that could see him comfortably through his senior years, and CBS's own desire to jump into the booming musical-instrument market at the height of Beatlemania.

By the end of this furtive year of corporate strategizing and dealmaking, Fender entered a new era, and the Stratocaster began what is generally recognized as a period of slow decline. If not responsible for any drastic identifiable changes in quality within its first few years, the CBS era was eventually perceived as having ushered in the lowest ebb for the Stratocaster by the mid- to late-1970s (and for Fender guitars and amplifiers in general), although the brand itself remained the choice of countless star players on the world's largest professional stages.

Jimi Hendrix plays an Olympic White Stratocaster with a telltale CBS-era headstock at London's Royal Albert Hall in 1969.

Leo Looks to Cash In

Although he was clearly still a visionary in the industry in which he'd pioneered one groundbreaking invention after another for nearly two decades, Leo Fender was also simply exhausted from the effort and badly in need of a total break from the grind. A perpetual burner of the midnight oil and constantly driven to develop new and better products, Leo was the type that might simply be branded a "workaholic" today, and by early 1964, those tendencies were exacerbating his existing health issues. He had been fighting a strep infection contracted in the mid-'50s that continually aggravated his sinuses, leaving him even more exhausted in his role atop the thriving guitar and amp maker.

Fender Sales, Inc., head Don Randall later expressed his awareness that Leo was becoming more and more burned out with the effort and that the two had begun discussing the possibility of selling the company as early as the start of 1964.

"[Leo] said, 'Well, Don, I think I ought to get a million and a half dollars now,'" Randall recalled many years later. To which he replied, "Well, that's probably not too far off. . . . Why don't I go ahead and see what I can do with the companies?"[1]

Leo gave the thumbs-down to the notion of going public on the stock market after Randall's preliminary talks with Merrill Lynch, so his business partner pursued an all-out purchase by a corporation large enough to pay top dollar. Following an approach by Baldwin, which Randall turned down, Merrill Lynch made an introduction to CBS, and negotiations ensued.

Come the 1960s, CBS—which is to say, the parent company Columbia Broadcasting System, Inc.—was a massive corporation with several arms in the entertainment industry. The television broadcaster was home to hits such as *The Ed Sullivan Show*, *The Andy Griffith Show*, *Gomer Pyle*, and *The Beverly Hillbillies*, and those in charge of expanding the holdings apparently had deep pockets heading into an acquisition spree in early 1964. On November 2, 1964, CBS paid $11.2 million to acquire an 80 percent stake in the New York Yankees baseball team, and by then talks were already underway with Don Randall to purchase Fender in its entirety.

Toward the end of 1964, a price of $13 million was set. The fine print on the contract was hammered out just before the close of the year, and the deal was finalized on January 5, 1965. Equivalent to more than $125 million today, the sum was the largest ever paid for a musical instrument company and certainly represented a little more than the "million and a half dollars" that Leo had supposed he could get for Fender.

CBS brought Fender in as a division of its Columbia Records Distribution Corporation and immediately renamed it Fender Musical Instruments, a change which is more noticeable on post-CBS amplifiers, which lost the "Electric" from their front and rear panels. Leo Fender and Don Randall were both retained on five-year contracts, Leo as a consultant in R&D and Randall as vice president and general manager. Both were also tied to ten-year noncompete clauses.

Apparently in a bid to fulfill his original quest for more R&R than R&D, Leo used a portion of his own proceeds from the sale to buy a large oceangoing boat, which he and his wife, Esther, frequently took between mainland California and Catalina Island. All reports indicate he spent very little time in the factory, while Randall busied himself with the demands of his position, traveling frequently between the California facility and his corporate office in the CBS building in New York City. Other key pre-CBS personnel and middle-management employees also made the jump to CBS, including Bill Carson, George Fullerton, Freddie Tavares, and Forrest White, although White was bumped to the position of plant manager since Randall had been given his former "general manager" title.

Some people close to Leo Fender in the 1950s and early 1960s have indicated that he might have been led to believe that his health was in more dire straits than it actually was, through misdiagnosis or some other general misunderstanding. Taking this to the extreme, there are reports that he might even have believed his illness to be terminal, or serious enough to make him unable to maintain his workaday grind for much longer.

Having suffered the affliction for nearly two decades, however, and after selling his company as a means of reducing the mounting stress and exhaustion, Leo found a new doctor who successfully diagnosed and treated the condition. "About 1968, I found a doctor who knew the appropriate treatment for the infection," he later told *Guitar Player* magazine, "and I haven't been bothered with it since."[2]

RIGHT: *A letter from the attorney for Leo and Don and their wives, requesting payment upon closing.* **BELOW:** *Canceled checks from CBS for $5,735,000 and $5,265,000 to the Fenders and the Randalls, respectively.* **BOTTOM:** *Leo Fender on vacation in the mid-'60s. With part of his proceeds from the sale, Leo bought a boat which he enjoyed cruising off the California coast.* **OPPOSITE:** *Leo Fender (left) and Don Randall (right), photographed around the time of the sale to CBS.*

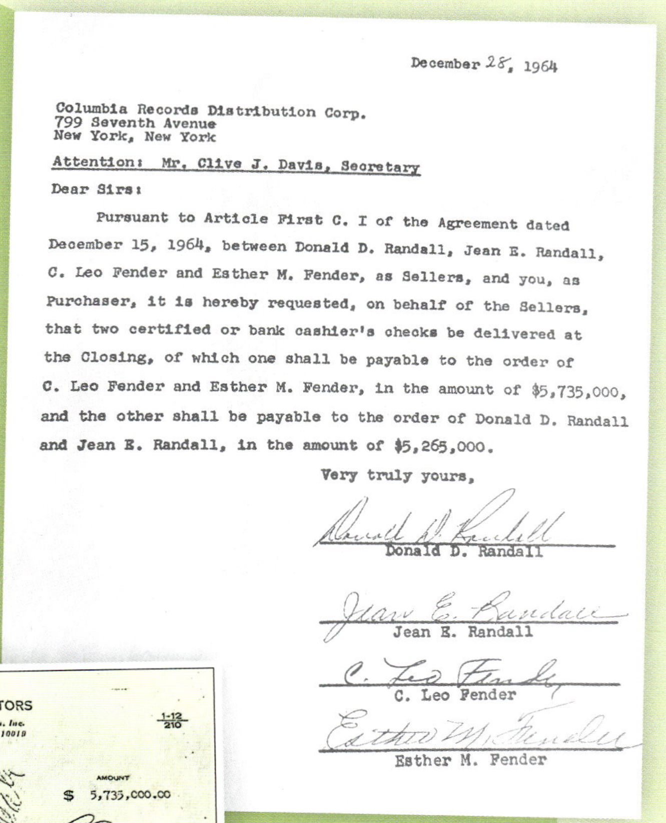

December 28, 1964

Columbia Records Distribution Corp.
799 Seventh Avenue
New York, New York

Attention: Mr. Clive J. Davis, Secretary

Dear Sirs:

Pursuant to Article First C. I of the Agreement dated December 15, 1964, between Donald D. Randall, Jean E. Randall, C. Leo Fender and Esther M. Fender, as Sellers, and you, as Purchaser, it is hereby requested, on behalf of the Sellers, that two certified or bank cashier's checks be delivered at the Closing, of which one shall be payable to the order of C. Leo Fender and Esther M. Fender, in the amount of $5,735,000, and the other shall be payable to the order of Donald D. Randall and Jean E. Randall, in the amount of $5,265,000.

Very truly yours,

Donald D. Randall

Jean E. Randall

C. Leo Fender

Esther M. Fender

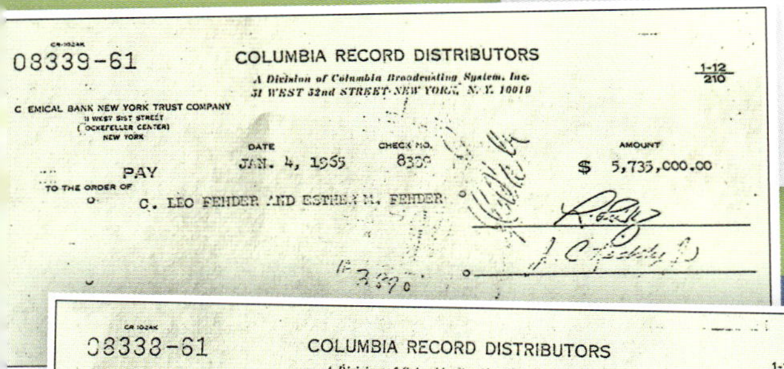

08339-61
COLUMBIA RECORD DISTRIBUTORS
A Division of Columbia Broadcasting System, Inc.
31 WEST 52nd STREET NEW YORK, N.Y. 10019
DATE JAN. 4, 1965
AMOUNT $ 5,735,000.00
PAY TO THE ORDER OF C. LEO FENDER AND ESTHER M. FENDER

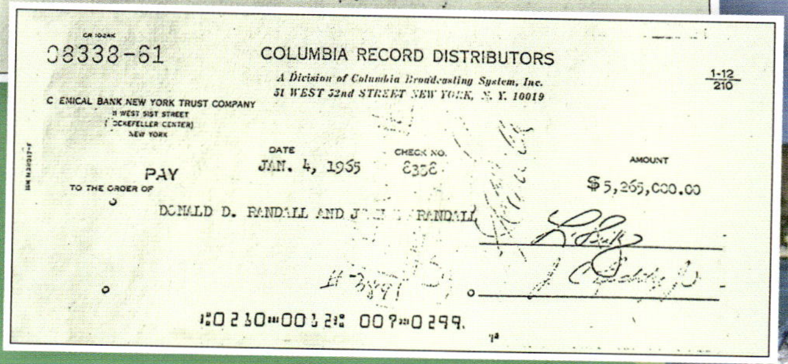

08338-61
COLUMBIA RECORD DISTRIBUTORS
A Division of Columbia Broadcasting System, Inc.
31 WEST 52nd STREET NEW YORK, N.Y. 10019
DATE JAN. 4, 1965
AMOUNT $5,265,000.00
PAY TO THE ORDER OF DONALD D. RANDALL AND J... RANDALL

Transitional Changes

Although the time frame between the end of '64 and start of '65 provides an accurate demarcation point between Fender's pre-CBS era and the major-corporate ownership that defined the brand for the next twenty years, the deeper changes that decreased the quality of Fender guitars and amplifiers wouldn't begin to bite for a few years. Several cosmetic changes were brought in quickly, and indeed some had already been enacted (as described in chapter 5), but for at least a few years these were relatively superficial as far as the Stratocaster was concerned. Several of the changes help us date guitars to the early CBS era and can provide fascinating historical footnotes.

Players and collectors have often pointed to the so-called "transition logo" as a sign of an early-CBS Stratocaster that retains features otherwise tied to the late pre-CBS era. Defining the logo itself in this manner, however, can be somewhat misleading. After his agency took over Fender advertising in 1957, Robert Perine noticed the company was using a handful of different logo styles for different applications, a practice he felt was detrimental to the brand's overall style. All guitars had worn the iconic pre-CBS "spaghetti logo"—so called for its narrow cursive font—but other logos appeared on a wide range of Fender products and marketing materials.

Perine set about designing a new logo featuring a wider gold cursive font with a thin black outline, and the look was made official a good six or seven years before it began appearing on the Strat's headstock. As he wrote many years later in 1997, "[T]he 40-year-old Fender logo got its initial approval back in 1958 in

TOP: *A gold "transition logo" adorns a Stratocaster with early maple-cap fingerboard.* **ABOVE LEFT AND RIGHT:** *This 1966 Stratocaster in Teal Green displays the gold logo on the newly enlarged headstock.* **OPPOSITE:** *Four Custom Color 1965 Stratocasters with thicker gold "transition-era" logos rest against a brown-panel Bassman amp from earlier in the decade.*

Leo's modest little lab. Fender Sales immediately adapted my design for promotional materials, but the factory took almost four years to use up the old decals and name plates. Leo, it seems, could not abide waste."[3] Part of the new logo design included Leo Fender's insistence that the first letter in the brand name should not, in fact, be written as a traditional "F" but as a "German 7," which appears much as an upper-case "F" written backwards.

The new logo, however, did appear on Fender instruments quite a bit earlier than Perine indicates. It debuted on the new Jazz Bass of 1960 and was applied to the Jaguar model introduced in 1962. It's a detail rarely noted, but although the Jaguar was a pre-CBS Fender model for the first three years of its existence, it never carried the spaghetti logo that Stratocaster guitars and Telecasters continued to wear at that time.

Stratocaster guitars wore the new logo almost universally from early 1965, although there are examples of late-1964 guitars that also carry it. As ever, though, accurately pinpointing a Fender guitar's birthdate is nearly impossible given the confluence of neck and body dates, dates stamped or written on other components, and the sequence of the neck-plate serial number that all come together to approximate a date of completion. Further complicating the supposed existence of late-'64 Strats with transition logos is the fact that the application of the headstock decal was one of the final steps before the completion of any guitar, whereas neck dates were stamped at the time the neck was completed, which could be months before the guitar came together as a whole.

Despite its initial use several years before the CBS era, Perine's new logo eventually was replaced in 1967 with a thick black logo with a thin gold outline in a similar font. This final CBS-era logo brought with it a much larger point size for the "Stratocaster" model name, now in all-caps and bold black.

Another change often viewed as an early-CBS spec is the replacement of the rosewood fingerboard's off-white clay dots with pearloid dots. Although the clay-dot feature remains desirable to players and collectors seeking pre-CBS Stratocaster guitars, the pearloid was clearly considered an upgrade by Fender and a means of eliminating the "dirty" look the off-white clay could take on from hours of finger smudging, leaving them harder to see on a dark stage. As with the bold gold logos, however, some pearl-dot Strats can be found with neck dates as early as the fall of 1964, making this mishmash of transitional elements, well, all the more transitional.

Necks with large headstocks are fitted with rosewood-fingerboards in the Fender factory in 1966.

The Large Headstock

Toward the end of 1965, Fender enlarged the headstock on the Stratocaster, a change often regarded as marking the end of the transitional period (although these would still wear the Perine logo for a time) and the beginning of the CBS-era Strat. This was not a dramatic change in some respects, making it a little under half an inch wider when measured at the broadest point (from the top edge just below the A-string tuner post to the bottom edge at the peak of the curved "point"), but it signaled a tectonic shift in aesthetics in the eyes of many aficionados.

Legend has it that the change was made to establish a larger template for the enlarged Fender logo, making it easier to recognize on stage and on TV—in other words, the type of executive decision we might expect from the corporate-minded CBS desk jockeys taking over the show at Fender. Such thinking, however, ignores the fact that an enlarged headstock that's closer to this new design than it is to that of the pre-CBS Stratocaster had already featured on the Jazzmaster from its introduction in 1958, and on the Jaguar from its arrival in 1962. These were not identical to the CBS-era Stratocaster headstock but were certainly larger than the original "small" Stratocaster headstock.

In any case, the arrival of the larger headstock on the Stratocaster has long been considered by many as emblematic of the general decline of the model in terms of quality and desirability. Yet this was the Stratocaster of Ritchie Blackmore, Jimi Hendrix, David Gilmour (well before the arrival of his famous #0001 Stratocaster in the late 1970s), and countless other stars of the era. Other than this extra bit of wood at the top, and the few other cosmetic alterations already addressed here and in chapter 5, a late-'65 or '66 Stratocaster was little different than a verifiably pre-CBS Strat of late '63 or early '64 and was still undeniably a great electric guitar by any measure.

(CONTINUED ON PAGE 132)

ABOVE: *A Blonde 1969 Stratocaster shows the model's features before major changes to come in the early '70s.* **OPPOSITE:** *For some, the larger headstock was associated with a general decline in quality. Yet these guitars were used by lauded players like David Gilmour and Ritchie Blackmore, to name but two.*

THIS PAGE: *A Blonde 1969 Stratocaster and a gold '71 display the model's specifications prior to significant changes later in 1971.* OPPOSITE: *A worker in the shipping department sports the casual couture of 1966, although the Fender box still displays the company's outdated pre-CBS "spaghetti" logo of a previous era.*

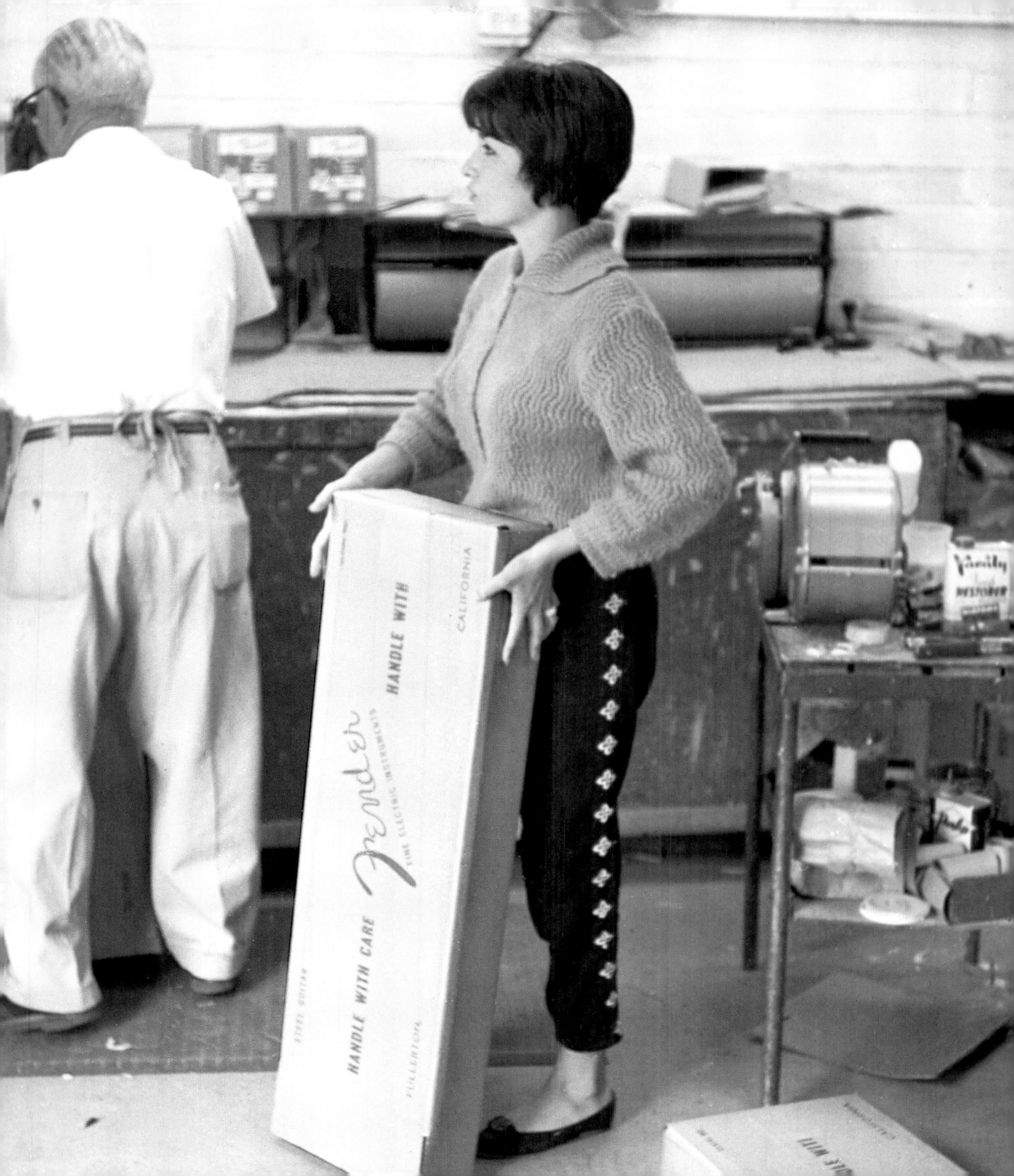
Fender
FINE ELECTRIC INSTRUMENTS
HANDLE WITH CARE
HANDLE WITH
CALIFORNIA
FULLERTON
STEEL GUITAR

Defining the Decline

Regardless of the quality retained by early CBS-era Stratocaster guitars, the model undeniably entered a period of significant changes that would culminate in a raft of nearly universally derided alterations enacted in the early 1970s. Some were introduced gradually, others simultaneously, but the sum of these changes was finally defined by the Stratocaster of, for example, late 1971 as a lesser guitar than its predecessors of 1954 to 1965.

In their ongoing efforts to pinpoint the Stratocaster's decline, many aficionados (having now generally agreed that it didn't happen overnight after the sale to CBS) point to the move to polyester finishes about three years after the sale. In 1968 Fender began using a polyester formulation for the bulk of the finishing process, applied atop a grain-filling undercoat (often a Fuller O'Brien product called Fullerplast from 1963 onward), with a topcoat of nitrocellulose lacquer over the main color coats. It's worth noting that headstock faces were still sprayed in nitro only because the decal failed to adhere properly to polyester.

Most likely the change in finishing process represented an effort to apply a more durable and lasting finish less prone to the checking, wearing, and flaking that might lead to warranty claims for former nitro finishes. The point against the polyester finish, though,

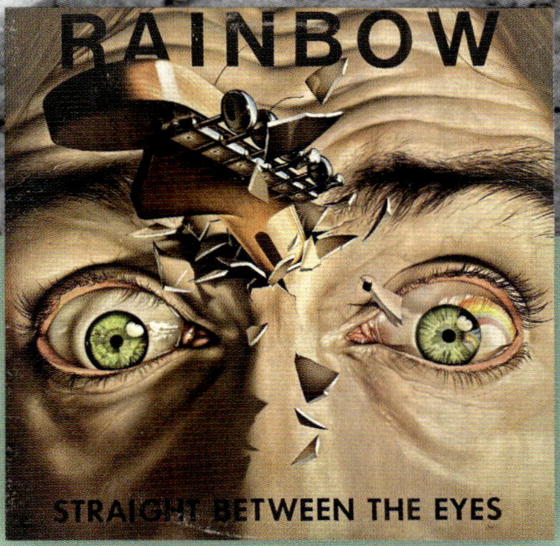

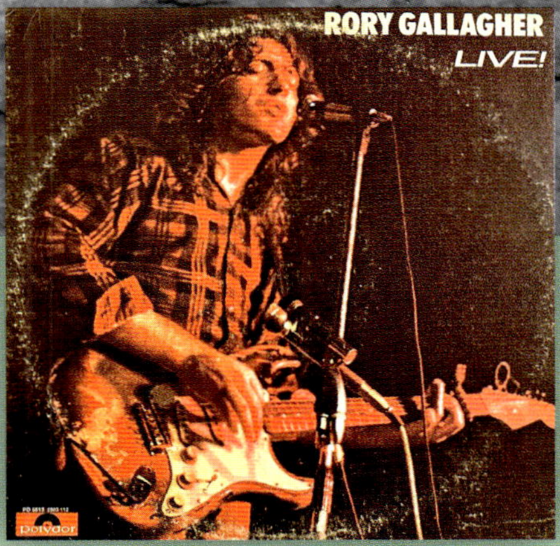

TOP AND OPPOSITE: *The newly enlarged Fender factory, circa 1966.* **RIGHT:** *Much like the players, Stratocasters often became "stars" in their own right, featuring prominently on album sleeves.*

The thicker polyester finish of the era is evident in the look of this Blonde Stratocaster, particularly in the texture of the slight ding on the body edge beneath the switch.

according to fans of pre-CBS guitars, is that its thicker nature is widely believed to dampen a guitar's natural resonance.

Many luthiers today agree that it's not the formulation of the finish that contributes to a resonant guitar but how thick it is applied. Existing Stratocaster guitars from 1968 to 1970 indicate the polyester coats were applied relatively thin, but a move to much thicker polyester finishes in the early '70s gave those late-'60s finishes a bad name with some players. From around 1971 onward, Fender sprayed its guitars with a "thick-skin finish," as it boasted in promotional literature, which did indeed provide a durable and high-gloss surface; but it yielded a plasticky playing feel that many guitarists have rebelled against.

The most significant changes to the Stratocaster's hardware and construction were enacted in the fall of 1971. At that time, a new three-screw neck attachment with tilt adjustment facility was introduced—with "Fender Micro-Neck-Adjust Patent 3550496" engraved on the neck plate—along with a headstock-end truss-rod adjustment nut shaped like a chromed bullet (hence the nickname "bullet headstock" that later stuck with these '70s Strats). In theory, these might have been considered innovations: the Micro-Neck-Adjust eliminated the need to place a shim in the neck pocket to achieve a steeper angle and thus a proper set-up, and the bullet headstock abolished the need to remove the neck to make truss-rod adjustments.

Furthermore, the three-screw neck attachment was one of Leo Fender's own developments, as would be seen on the early guitars made by the G&L company he formed with George Fullerton in 1980 (G&L eventually moved to a four-screw attachment, but ironically, the earlier three-bolt G&L guitars are now often more highly prized). On the ground and in the hands of guitarists, however, these became the telltale signs of '70s Stratocaster guitars considered plagued by a broad and overarching decline in quality.

Later that same year, Fender replaced the vibrato bridge's cold-rolled steel inertia block and bent-steel saddles—originally designed by Leo and Freddie Tavares—with parts made from diecast Mazak (a.k.a. Zamak). This pot-metal alloy of zinc, aluminum, magnesium, and copper made for cheaper and easier component fabrication, but many guitarists found it detrimental to the Stratocaster's sustain and resonance, inducing a tonal alteration often described as "thinner" or "lighter."

And, as if all of this wasn't enough, Fender Stratocaster guitars of the 1970s represent some of the heaviest examples in the model's history. The drive to max out production numbers, and to minimize the unit costs, led to the use of wood supplies of lesser and lesser quality. The design that had most often been made with a two-piece body in years past was now often carved from blanks put together from three, four, or even more pieces of wood glued together vertically from tail to neck pocket.

Finally, in a less consequential move, though one still noted by collectors, the legend "with Synchronized Tremolo" was dropped from the Stratocaster's headstock logo in 1971.

However you look at it, the Fender Stratocaster of the pre-CBS years and up into the late 1960s was an undeniable classic. By the end of 1971, however, a Strat just didn't sound quite the same as one that had rolled off the line at the start of the year. In fact, that single year between the start and end of 1971 arguably represented the most dramatic change in the specifications and components of the Stratocaster in the model's history. Considering the massive free publicity Fender was handed by Jimi Hendrix's use of the Stratocaster from 1967 until his death in 1970, we might see this as an ill-considered downgrading of a guitar that was potentially at its peak otherwise.

(CONTINUED ON PAGE 139)

ABOVE: *Musicians continued to create and perform groundbreaking music on Stratocasters during the CBS era, both with pre- and post-1965 instruments. Glam rocker Marc Bolan (left) tears up Wembley in 1972 with one of his Olympic White models, and Irish bluesman Rory Gallagher (right) is seen in 1973 with his famous 1961 Stratocaster.* OPPOSITE: *Major changes of late 1971 included the three-screw neck plate and die-cast bridge saddles.*

398634
FENDER MICRO-NECK-ADJUST PAT. 3550496

Fender
STRATOCASTER
NORMAL
VOLUME
TREBLE
BASS
REVERB
SPEED
INTENSITY
VIBROLUX ®
REVERB
VOLUME
TONE
TONE

Randall's Retreat

Having been so instrumental to Fender's success overall, and having helmed the sale to CBS in particular, Don Randall's view of the changes through the mid- to late-'60s puts the situation into a finer focus. Randall would later say time and again that the overall quality of Fender guitars changed very little in the first few years of CBS oversight, but come the end of the decade, he perceived a noticeable slide.

"CBS did so many things," he said in a 1992 interview with author Tony Bacon, "if I may say so, stupid things. They took some of our equipment that we'd paid a whole lot of money for, and because they didn't really know how to operate it, they put it out in the back lot and let it rust and go to pot. Thousands and thousands of dollars of specialized equipment."[4]

Speaking further on the matter, Randall recalled in a 2006 interview for the NAMM Oral Histories project,

Everything seemed to start falling apart. . . . When they were dickering with me to buy the company they were gung-ho about everything, and they were the first two years that I ran the company for them. It came out pretty well. Then they got all these idiots that they had working for them in New York started finding excuses to come out to the West Coast, you know, big trip. It just screwed up the whole detail. It finally made me sick to my stomach. . . . Nice enough guys as individuals, but when it came to something like this, here they're coming out of the broadcasting business and sticking their nose in the music business. They didn't know a thing about it. It was just disgusting.[5]

Having become more and more disillusioned and dissatisfied with the operation under CBS, Randall departed the company in 1969, several months before the official end of his five-year contract as vice president and general manager.

Without Randall, Fender forged on under CBS through the 1970s and into the 1980s and remained a huge business that sold a lot of guitars, although many players on the scene at the time—not to mention those later who benefited from hindsight—felt that a Stratocaster of 1977 was not the same instrument as a Stratocaster made in 1957. Nevertheless, a wealth of great and groundbreaking music was still made on Strats manufactured during the CBS years, even though many guitarists were already regarding the era as the nadir of the model's existence.

A post-changes early-1970s Stratocaster rests on a Deluxe Reverb amp of the same era.

Fender promotions of the 1970s stepped up into the styles of the day.

The world's favorite flying machine
Fender
Musical Instruments

Chapter 7

A REBIRTH, AND BACK TO BASICS

Adapting to Evolving Styles

The 1970s marked a period of rapidly changing styles and evolving technologies throughout the music industry, and Fender spent much of that era striving to stay in step with the trends. The decade opened with the coalescing of the heavily overdriven guitar as the central sound of big-time rock—often epitomized by humbucking pickups into British full-stack amps on huge arena stages—and ended with the rebellious transition through punk rock in one direction and the electronic music's threat to bury the guitar on the other.

Jeff Beck performs at the Music Hall, in Boston, on May 3, 1975. The 1970s would find Fender eventually pivoting back to the basics.

Rise of the Superstrat

While contemplating everything the Stratocaster *was* through the course of its history, it's sometimes interesting to contemplate what it *wasn't*. Despite the general craze for modifying guitars to add humbuckers, the Stratocaster never officially got one. Even so, the concept of the "superstrat"—a Strat-shaped guitar (though often by another maker), usually with at least one humbucker and a deluxe "locking" vibrato bridge—was becoming common in the guitar world in the mid-'70s, in concept if not always in name.

Eddie Van Halen is likely the most famous early proponent of the craze, exploding onto the scene in 1978 with a humbucker in the bridge position of his heavily modified "Frankenstrat," which was not a Fender guitar at all but certainly patterned after the iconic bolt-neck double-cutaway design. Others too numerous to name had already trodden that ground before him for several years, although these one-offs generally included the humbucker modification without the addition of a locking vibrato.

Wayne Kramer of the MC5 was seen sporting a humbucking pickup in the middle position of his "American flag" Stratocaster as early as 1970, while Ritchie Blackmore, already responsible for some of the most powerful Strat-based tones in the rock world, had at least one of his Stratocaster guitars modified around 1974 to carry two humbucking pickups. And as if to one-up him, Michael Hampton toured with Parliament Funkadelic in 1975 and 1976 wielding a modified Stratocaster with *three* humbuckers in it.

Fender wouldn't officially put a humbucker in a Strat until the Japanese-made Contemporary Stratocaster of 1984, which also had a modernized locking vibrato bridge and locking nut, but we're getting ahead of ourselves.

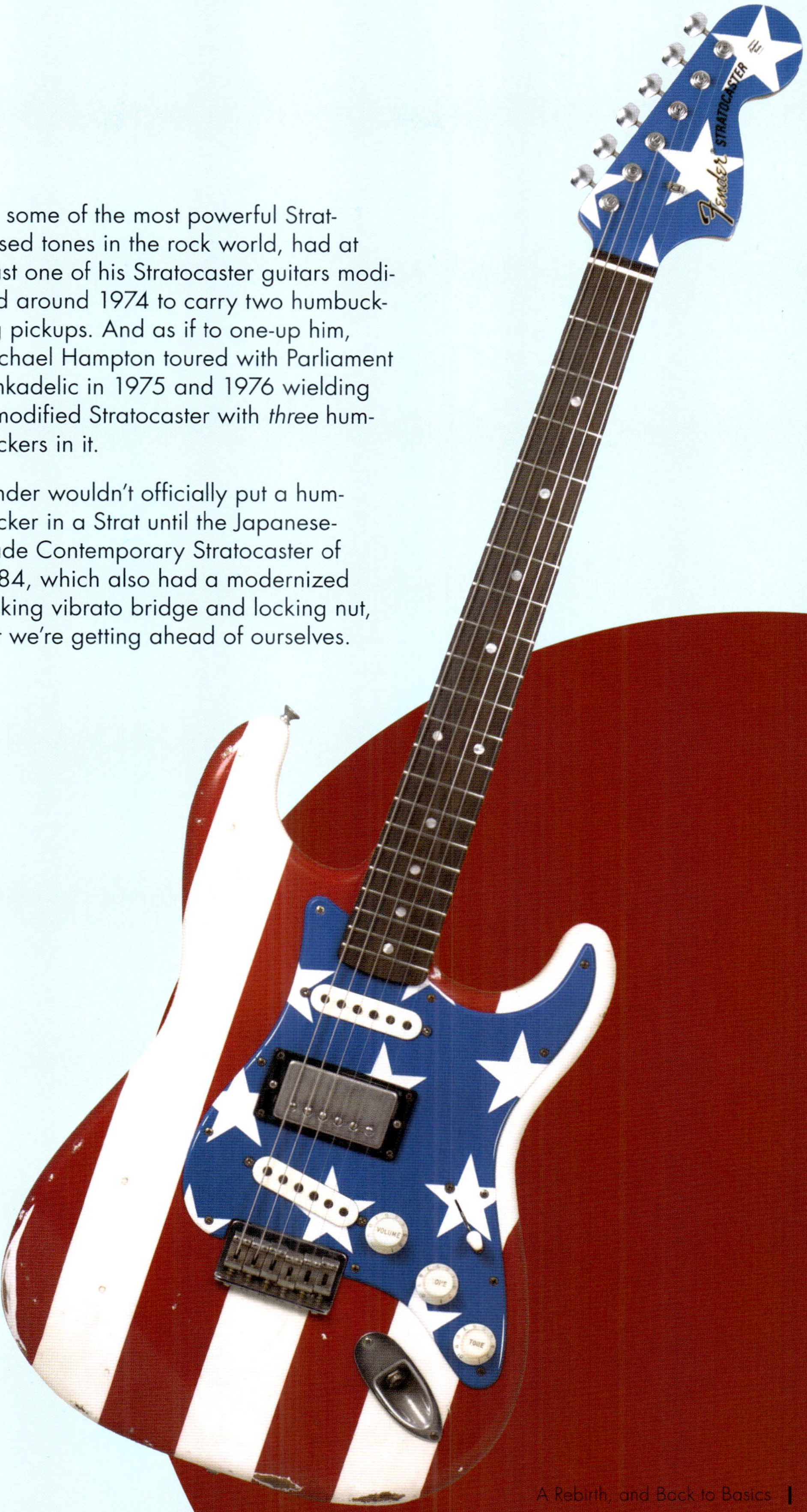

Brother Wayne Kramer of the MC5 epitomized the '70s craze for installing a full-size humbucker in a Stratocaster, albeit wedging one into the middle position in his case. The guitar was resurrected with the 2010 Signature edition also seen here.

Fender Makes a Humbucker

Although the Stratocaster had been used to make some of the heaviest rock heard up to that time, many players were chasing the thick sound of the humbucking pickup, and Fender felt the need to deliver its own rendition. It's interesting to consider that although the Stratocaster had become heavy rockers' clear choice from the Fender stable, and some had already taken it upon themselves to rout out their Strats and install a humbucking pickup in the bridge position, Fender hadn't offered a stock model thus equipped. In fact, until the late '70s, Fender never offered any variation whatsoever on the Stratocaster as a standard model.

The Telecaster, on the other hand, was subjected to five alternative formats between 1959 and 1972, not including the single-pickup Esquire variations. Following the release of the Telecaster Custom with bound body in 1959, Fender introduced the semihollow Telecaster Thinline in 1968, revamped it heavily in 1971, and then also revamped the Custom in 1972 and introduced the Telecaster Deluxe that same year. The last three of these Telecaster variations all carried Fender's own humbucking pickup.

Gibson's own full-size humbucker of 1957 onward had been designed in part by Seth Lover, an engineer who came to work for Fender in 1967. Tasked with taking the Fullerton company into the humbucking age—retaining the classic "Fender sound" while doing so—Lover had a unit ready to go by 1970: the Wide Range Humbucking Pickup. To retain that seminal clear, bright Fender sound, Lover used molded Cunife magnet polepieces within the dual coils rather than following the Gibson formula of steel polepieces with a magnet mounted below them. The result was a pickup that was more powerful than Fender's single-coil units of the day but had a sparkling, articulate sound that still allied it to the company's sonic signature. Yet it was never used in the Stratocaster.

LEFT: *Fender's 1976 Starcaster semi-acoustic was a good candidate for a pair of Wide Range Humbucking Pickups. The model ran from 1976 to 1979.*
RIGHT: *The Telecaster Thinline was the first guitar to receive Fender's new Wide Range humbucker in 1971.*

Revised Specs and Special Editions

Although his superiors wouldn't have realized it at the time, twenty-one-year-old John Page's hiring as a neck buffer on the shop floor in 1978 signaled the arrival of one of several new talents who would eventually help to put Fender back on its feet and possibly save it altogether. Starting in a lower-level manufacturing position, Page worked hard and moved up the ranks quickly to bring a revised perspective to Fender's design and manufacturing efforts just when it was needed most.

Meanwhile, it was already becoming clear toward the end of the decade that some sort of major shake-up was needed. Sales and production had continued to increase dramatically throughout the early to mid-1970s, such that any "number cruncher" observing from the outside would deem Fender a considerable success: CBS built an enormous new five-acre facility in Fullerton in 1976 where more than 750 people were then employed; by 1979 Fender was selling forty thousand guitars a year; and in 1980 the company had tripled the $20-million-a-year income that Don Randall had boasted about a decade before. Yet something was clearly and drastically wrong with the formula, and sales and profits were on the verge of declining rapidly. Through the '70s, CBS had reinvested little of the profits into maintaining production standards at Fender, and for all the sales and income, the company was losing money by the early '80s.

To help streamline the guitar range, Fender deleted the Mustang, Bronco, Telecaster Deluxe, and Telecaster

Custom from the lineup and ditched the short-lived Starcaster, a semihollow electric design with dual Wide Range humbuckers that ran from 1976 to 1979. The Jaguar had already been dropped in 1974, and the Jazzmaster went the way of the dodo in 1980. A greater concentration on the core models included the introduction of several variations on the Stratocaster format, including the Antigua Stratocaster in 1977, the limited-edition Silver Anniversary Stratocaster in 1979, the "Strat" model in 1980, and the limited-edition Hendrix Stratocaster in 1980 (*very* limited at twenty-five units and often referred to as the "Hendrix Stratocaster prototype" because of its scant availability).

This flurry of special editions, plus one take on a modern alternative, signals that Fender was putting a lot of stock in the Stratocaster in general. A deeper look at these models also reveals that the personnel in the R&D department felt some return to pre-CBS specs might help the cause. Excluding the Antigua Stratocaster, which mainly brought with it a special color scheme, the 1979–1980 period represents the first time Fender offered *any* variation on a Stratocaster's features and construction that deviated from the standard flagship model in that year's catalog (Custom Colors and maple/rosewood fretboard options aside).

The 25th Anniversary Stratocaster, the Strat, and the Hendrix Stratocaster all dispensed with the late-1971 CBS changes to the three-bolt Micro-Neck-Adjust attachment and bullet truss-rod adjustment nut on the headstock end, returning to four-bolt neck attachments and body-end truss-rod nuts. The Hendrix Stratocaster was devised by VP of sales and marketing Mudge Miller and designed largely by John Page, who had just been promoted to the design team. It also reintroduced elements of the pre-1971 vibrato bridge with bent-steel saddles.

But the Strat perhaps got the most attention for its revival of a slimmer Stratocaster headstock reminiscent of the pre-CBS design, albeit one not cut to a shape representative of the original, thanks to worn-out or misplaced tooling.

THIS PAGE: *The 1979 Silver Anniversary Stratocaster (left) was emblematic of an increased focus on core models beginning in the late 1970s, while the Strat model (right) encapsulated the state of the design circa 1980.*
OPPOSITE: *A young John Page at his bench in the R&D department confers with Fender legend Freddie Tavares.*

The "Dan Smith" Stratocaster Bridges a Vintage Revival

Although the Strat headstock revision had missed the mark slightly, there's plenty of evidence from several fronts in the late '70s and early '80s that many members of the team saw a return to the company's glory days in the '50s and '60s as the best way forward. In his new role on the design team, Page was tasked with introducing a new student line to the Fender catalog, which resulted in the acclaimed Bullet Series of 1981. Soon after this, though, he was tapped to help in the quest to reclaim vintage-correct specifications for the leading models. Working alongside Freddie Tavares, and with support from marketing manager Paul Bugielski, Page had already begun the effort to improve the quality of Fender's guitars—instilling measures such as improved finish-curing systems and insisting on returning to original templates and tooling to achieve consistent body and neck shapes and contours—and their efforts were about to get a significant boost from the top.

Part of the conscious effort to restore the company's reputation included CBS's hiring of a trio of young executives in 1981. Fresh from the US branch of Japanese instrument maker Yamaha, which was enjoying major success with its SG2000 and other electric guitars, Bill Schultz, John McLaren, and Dan Smith hit the ground running in their quest to revise the product line—starting with the Stratocaster—but they found they had some obstacles to overcome.

"We took it for granted that they could make Stratocaster guitars and Telecasters the way they used to make them," Smith recalled. "But we were wrong. So many things had been changed in the plant."[1]

Similarly, Schultz later recalled, "CBS allowed the company to deteriorate—the products, the quality. But when I took over, they gave me millions of dollars to put back into R&D, to put into equipment, and we brought the quality level back up."[2]

Major players of the day were still wholeheartedly embracing earlier Fender guitars and amplifiers, and fans and hobbyists wanted to follow in their footsteps. British guitarist Mark Knopfler had reintroduced the compelling tone of a distortion-free Stratocaster to the world via several big hits with his band Dire Straits, and Stevie Ray Vaughan was reigniting the blues scene on a battered '62 Stratocaster. Vintage specs and quality were where it was at, and the new team devised a plan to get Fender back there.

In the team's first bid to reestablish the Strat's reputation, Smith devised a new Standard Stratocaster that built upon the reassessment of vintage specs while adding new features that contemporary players might appreciate. Often referred to today as the "Dan Smith" Stratocaster, these guitars were made in Fullerton from 1981 until partway through 1983. They featured a somewhat more accurate smaller headstock shape, though one that still wore the bold CBS-era logo (the last few made in '83 would carry a revised Fender logo), four-bolt neck attachment and body-end truss-rod adjustment, and the same hotter X-1 single-coil pickup in the bridge position that had debuted in the Strat the year before. Although it was produced for less than three years, the "Dan Smith" Stratocaster helped carry Fender through a period of major reassessment of the Strat's features and specifications, and also pointed the way toward one of latter-day Fender's most significant models: the American Standard Stratocaster.

Meanwhile, Smith was also enlisting the assistance of Page and others in the pursuit of the Vintage Reissue Series. The race was on to build a Stratocaster "like they did in the old days."

"Dan Smith and I traveled to a big vintage guitar store in Illinois to check out as many vintage Fenders guitars as we could," recalled Page. "We recorded lots of specs, took tons of photos, and bought several to bring back to the factory with us."[3] The results marked the beginning of Fender's vigorous Vintage Reissue program and in many ways signaled the wholesale revival of the company itself—although there were plenty of stumbles and road-blocks to come before the brand returned to its former glory.

Page's R&D mentor, Freddie Tavares, had been working on a vintage-spec 1952 Telecaster Reissue, which would be joined by the team's '57 Stratocaster with maple fingerboard and '62 Stratocaster with rosewood fingerboard to comprise the new Vintage Reissue Series. Launched with production in both the US and at the FujiGen Gakki factory in Japan (the latter initially intended for the overseas domestic market only), the Japanese manufacturing got up to speed more quickly and hit the streets first, unlocking unforeseen potential of which Smith, Schultz, and McClaren quickly took advantage.

(CONTINUED ON PAGE 154)

A tasty gold example of the early-1980s model that has come to be known as a "Dan Smith" Stratocaster.

TOP: *Dan Smith and Bill Schultz join top Fender players. Back row (from left): Hal Lindes, Smith, Schultz, Jeff Beck, and David Gilmour. Front row (from left): Stuart Adamson, Eric Clapton, Hank Marvin, Steve Howe, and Richard Thompson.*
ABOVE: *The student-priced Bullet was John Page's first original design for Fender.*
OPPOSITE: *A 1984 American Vintage Reissue (AVRI) 1957 Stratocaster. The series was an attempt to build a Stratocaster "like they did in the old days."*
OPPOSITE TOP RIGHT: *Dan Smith (left) holds a then-new AVRI '57 Stratocaster.*

Vintage Series
'57 stratocaster
INSTRUCTION MANUAL
Fender
Fender

Fender

Japan Rising and Elite in America

Given the need for extensive retooling in Fullerton in 1982 to enable a proper run of American-made Vintage Reissue guitars, Fender initially began its production of similar models via Fender Japan Co. Ltd., which was founded in the spring of that same year. Originally intended only for Japanese and European markets, many found their way to the United States, and players were generally very impressed.

The early runs of these instruments carried the full-size Fender logo with "Squier Series" beneath it to distinguish the Japanese guitars. That was soon changed to a larger Squier logo, and then Squier by Fender a short while after. Although the venture was initially to buy the American Fender operation some breathing room to get back up and running under the new management, the Squier range introduced an enduring line of more affordable guitars that has had strong sales ever since. Early examples of Squier Stratocaster guitars are recognized for their quality, and many have become collectible in their own right.

American-made Vintage Reissue Stratocaster guitars emerged later that year, joining the '52 Telecaster Reissue that Tavares had spearheaded. Players generally received them enthusiastically, and early examples have become collector's items, valued as the last vintage-spec Stratocaster guitars made by Fender in Fullerton. There was turmoil yet to come at Fender itself—even if their specifications generally aren't quite as vintage-correct as later Vintage Reissues and Custom Shop renditions—but the maker had identified a viable path forward via this creative look backward, and the return of vintage-style Stratocaster guitars confirmed that countless players still wanted their Strats made "the old way."

Reflecting on the adventure four decades later, John Page gives an interesting first-hand perspective on that time of great change and reinvention at Fender:

TOP AND OPPOSITE: *A Fiesta Red 1983 Squier Stratocaster. The earliest Japanese Stratocasters carried a Fender logo with "Squier Series" decal at the headstock end.* RIGHT: *Squier transitioned into a brand unto itself, and a major success in Fender's lower-priced market.*

As a 24-year-old kid, I initially didn't realize the importance of being the lead designer of the Reissue Series back in the early 1980s. I had the mind of a designer, so I was looking to design new things, and to me the reissues were basically a documentation project of an old design. Granted, calls had to be made and processes developed, but there was nothing new from a design point of view, so I think I was looking at it selfishly to begin with. I didn't recognize the importance of what it meant to the Fender legacy or to my growth and understanding as a designer until sometime later.

Seeing the impact it had on the players around the world—the 'so glad to see Fender coming back' comments from everyone—that's when I realized the importance of the project and how fortunate I was to be a part of it. It's also when I realized that a lot of what was lost during Fender's less lustrous years was listening directly to players. Listening to players' needs drove Fender's early successful years, so it was a key lesson for me to learn. A lesson that was later instrumental in the creation of, and guiding principles of, the Custom Shop.[4]

Within the contemporary lineup of 1983, Fender introduced the Stratocaster Elite, a guitar that merged the company's rediscovery of the slimmer headstock and four-bolt neck joint with a plethora of modern, innovative features. Produced only through '84, the model wasn't regarded as a great success, but its use of active TBX tone and MDX mid-boost circuits, individual push-button switches for each pickup, and a unique top-mounted Freeflyte vibrato unit signaled a willingness to design forward-looking Strats for adventurous modern guitarists while embracing the undeniable appeal of the Vintage Reissue guitars.

Fender Seeks a New Owner . . . Again

In hindsight, the early 1980s denotes a significant refresh in the Stratocaster identity and an upturn in Fender quality in general, but these very notable steps forward didn't prove enough to keep CBS in the guitar business. Fender had lost money year upon year from 1981 to 1984 and had also cut its workforce from 700 to 275 in that time. By 1984 the big corporation had evidently grown weary of its place in the industry—despite taking Fender to new heights of sales and profitability, if not quality, just a few years before—and began looking for a buyer for the Fullerton operation, repeating the process Leo Fender and Don Randall had undertaken exactly twenty years before.

Unlike the sale of Fender to CBS in 1964, however, the guitar industry was in a very different place. Although Fender had continued to do big business through the 1970s, musical trends were continually threatening to put the guitar in the backseat in the early to mid-'80s. New Wave and post-punk had deglamorized the guitar hero, those that remained in popular music were often relegated to the spandex-and-hair-metal genres, and the synthesizer and electronic music kept promising to bury the guitar entirely. What's more, the general perception in the biz was that the Japanese makers were still eating the Americans' lunch. Rather than booming as it was in the mid-'60s, the guitar industry appeared on the back end of the curve, and few buyers were tripping over themselves to acquire the historic brand.

With no sizeable existing corporations making suitable offers, CBS asked those on the executive team if they'd like to raise the funds to purchase the company themselves. On March 5, 1985, CBS sold Fender for $12.5 million to a management group headed by Bill Schultz (who became CEO of the newly formed Fender Musical Instrument Company) and including Dan Smith and other Fender executives and investors. The purchase price was $500,000 less than CBS had paid for Fender two decades earlier (before adjusting for inflation), but the sale excluded most of the existing Fender machinery and many patents, as well as the 250,000-square-foot Fullerton factory itself, all of which were to be sold separately.

Setting out to build the company virtually from the ground up, and approximately $11 million in debt while doing so, the new owners had a major job on their hands—but seemingly boundless energy, creativity, and desire too. Some years later, Schultz recalled his rationale for taking the leap and purchasing the floundering company in the face of such long odds: "Fender has a great name, a great founder. All we had to do was follow his philosophy. We work under the premise that you've got to look ahead and make changes—you have to keep innovating, creating, and developing—but you can never forget your past. And our past was Leo Fender. It was a lot of fun to follow somebody like that."[5]

Mark Knopfler brought semi-clean Stratocaster tones back to the forefront in an era otherwise dominated by rock and punk.

SRV

Stevie Ray Vaughan sounded huge through his pre-CBS Stratocaster and a wall of amps—and reignited the blues in the process.

As successful as Fender would again become in the next three decades, it's difficult to conceive of the peril that the historic guitar maker was in at the time. An article in the *Los Angeles Times* announcing the impending sale succinctly summed up the situation:

> **CBS Inc. said Friday it has agreed in principle to sell its troubled Fender Musical Instruments unit—whose electric guitars have been a mainstay of today's popular music. . . . The proposed sale puts to rest speculation that Fender, a pioneer in modern electric music that has suffered in recent years from foreign competition and a shrinking guitar market, might be sold to a Japanese company or go out of business."[6]**

Schultz indicated at the time that Fender would have to cut its workforce again by more than half, down to 110, to weather the financial constraints. Meanwhile, without a factory to work in, any profits that could be made to get the new team on its feet would have to come from overseas production. Early in 1985, US manufacture of Fender instruments officially ceased, and the Japanese factory produced all Fender guitars between February and October 1985. It would seem a massive hole for Schultz, Smith, and the remaining team to dig out of—but dig they did.

ABOVE: *Influential Stratocaster-playing artists of the era made a point of featuring the guitar on their album art.* **LEFT:** *A later example of the American Standard Stratocaster—still a flagship model in the mid-2010s.*

Chapter 8

BEST OF THE BEST

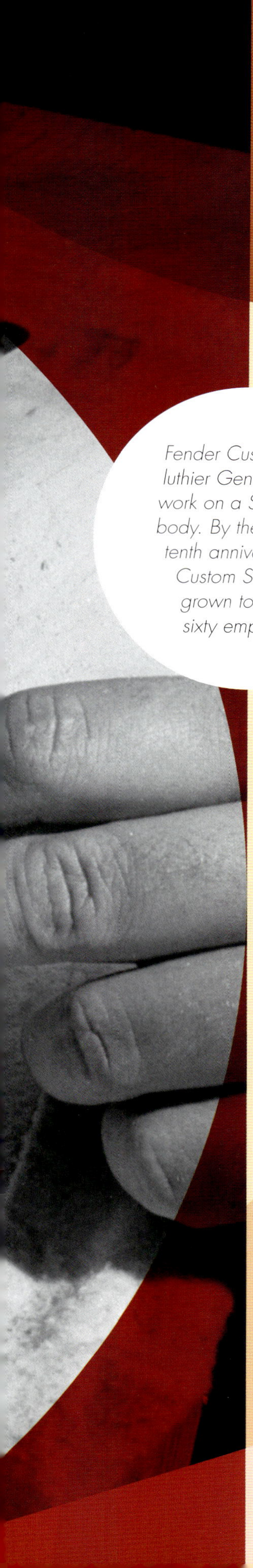

Fender Custom Shop luthier Gene Baker at work on a Stratocaster body. By the time of its tenth anniversary, the Custom Shop had grown to include sixty employees.

The Custom Shop

The energetic management team at Fender Musical Instrument Co. (FMIC)—now its new *owners*—had barely finished construction on a new manufacturing facility in Corona, California, when CEO Bill Schultz decided to take the company's return to quality up a notch further by establishing the Custom Shop. Players the world over have long relied on this elite department to deliver the finest new Fender guitars available anywhere, but in 1986, it was a new concept, and a radical venture at that.

Often the term "custom guitar" implies something special-order, made with unusual features and nonstandard specs. For Fender players, however, the Custom Shop often represents their best access to accurate renditions of the company's guitars of the '50s and '60s. In fact, the Fender Custom Shop was founded to make both period-correct vintage re-creations and one-off custom orders to suit any Fender-related desire.

Anticipating that the elite new department might be outstanding PR at best—possibly costing more money to run than it could bring in—Schultz tasked FMIC Vice President Dan Smith with hiring a team of top-notch luthiers and setting it up. On reflection, the Custom Shop appears to have swiftly gone from no premises or personnel to producing next-level electric guitars played by the biggest names in music, but it was undoubtedly a seat-of-the-pants thrill ride getting there. It didn't hurt that Fender landed two luthiers of unprecedented talent to get it rolling.

The Quiet Cowboy and the California Kid

Already a luthier to the stars by the mid-1980s and a genuine Texas cowboy to boot, Michael Stevens had been on Smith's radar even before Bill Schultz had broached the notion of a Fender Custom Shop. After learning his chops in Texas, Stevens jumped in at the deep end in 1967 as a repairman at the famed Guitar Resurrection shop in San Francisco under his mentor, Larry Jameson, doing maintenance and custom work for some of the Bay Area's most famous guitarists of the late '60s and early '70s.

After taking four years away from the guitar scene in the mid-'70s to train Arabian show horses back in his native Texas, he set up shop in Austin in 1978, making guitars for a veritable who's-who of the thriving music scene there, including Stevie Ray and Jimmie Vaughan, Otis Rush, Albert King, Eric Johnson, Lonnie Mack, Hubert Sumlin, Junior Brown, and others. A connection to Robben Ford via Stevens client and bassist Roscoe Beck brought the luthier into Dan Smith's sights at a NAMM show in the mid-1980s, and soon Smith was courting him for a role at Fender.

"It was in early '86," Stevens tells us, "after that NAMM show, that Dan [Smith] called about using me as a consultant, and again about licensing my design, and then about the Custom Shop concept—and finally about all three at once. Was I interested? Meanwhile, a Flying V I'd built won 'Best of Show' at the Dallas Guitar Show in 1986, and I got a call from Gibson about their Custom Shop, then run by Tim Shaw, an old friend of mine. I took the Fender job."[1]

Smith knew that setting up the Custom Shop would be a two-person job; he liked John Page in the second role and offered Stevens the right of approval of his cofounder. But there were two hitches in the plan: Page didn't currently work at Fender, and Stevens had never met him. Fortunately, both obstacles were easily overcome. After taking most of the year off to work on his own music following an intensive eight years since his start at Fender in 1978, Page was ready to return to the security of a day job. He contacted Smith: "Dan gave me the choice of going back into Guitar R&D, the position I had left in January, or working with Michael Stevens in the Custom Shop. Although we had discussed opening the Custom Shop many years prior, Bill had finally decided to make it happen. I thought that would be pretty cool, so I chose the latter."[2]

As a specialist in vintage guitars and an up-and-coming luthier to the stars, Stevens hadn't paid much attention to the workings of Fender under CBS, and he saw the advantage of having an insider at his side. That and Page's talent was immediately apparent. "Page and I hit it off quickly," he said, "and I realized I needed his knowledge of Fender. Done!"

LEFT: *The Custom Shop's founding master builders, John Page and Michael Stevens.*

BELOW: *Dan Smith with an early Custom Shop Stratocaster.*

Hit the Ground Running

Not unlike the push nearly thirty-four years before to get a Stratocaster prototype to NAMM quickly, Fender was eager to show off the new Custom Shop as soon as possible. And that meant taking several guitars to the 1987 Winter NAMM show just two months away. "In December of '86, I went to work in Austin getting Eric Johnson two American Standards ready for NAMM, since he was already a customer of mine," says Stevens. "They furnished lots of parts, necks, and bodies to choose from, refret, tweak. . . . When I got out there for NAMM, Alice [Stevens's late wife] went off to find a house and I went to work in a very cluttered R&D shop in Brea to start getting necks ready for the Eric Clapton model that was hopefully soon to happen."[3]

Page's account of their start reflects a similar state of hitting the ground running:

When Michael and I first started working in January of '87, we were in the R&D Model Shop in Brea. A small, fenced-off area in the warehouse just outside of the R&D offices. Fender needed us to build some guitars, and our "real" shop was yet to be built at the Corona factory. We only worked in there for a couple of weeks, as I recall, because then Michael had to leave to make the final move from Texas.

While he was gone, I worked with the Corona factory manager to get the construction going on our new shop, an 800-square-foot area walled off from the main factory floor. I also started buying tools that we would need for the shop. Michael was used to tools that were mostly suited for smaller shops, like hand routers and such, while I was used to factory-type tools, like pin routers. So, we had both. When he returned about a month or so later, we ended up working in his garage shop for a couple of months while waiting for the new facility to be completed. I think we complemented each other's knowledge and skill, so each of us learned from the other.[4]

LEFT: *A 1986 Eric Clapton Stratocaster, one of the Custom Shop's first artist guitars.* OPPOSITE: *A Custom Shop David Gilmour Stratocaster from 2016.*

The marriage of history and innovation that would propel the Custom Shop forever after was established by its first official guitar for a customer: a Stevens-built white Blonde double-neck that combined a Stratocaster and an Esquire, with gold-plated hardware. Built for Jimmy Wallace, guitarist with the band the Stratoblasters and producer of the Dallas Guitar Show and Music Festival, it was the first double-neck guitar ever produced and sold by Fender (prototypes excluded) and was given the serial number 0001.

Just a few months into its inception, it became clear to all involved that the Fender Custom Shop was becoming much more than even its founders had anticipated. "I'm particularly proud just to have gotten it jumpstarted and headed with pride in the right direction," Stevens later reflected. "Bill Schultz told me, 'If we can only break even, I want the coolest Custom Shop on the planet!' We did that and put Fender back on the map."[5]

On May 15, 1987, FMIC sent out the first official notice of the opening of the Custom Shop, which included a list of prices for various guitars and services. By August, just three months after Fender had made it official, Stevens and Page had more than three hundred orders, an impossible backlog for two builders to fulfill. The team would have to grow. And grow it did.

Far beyond "breaking even," the Custom Shop quickly showed its ability to make a profit. In addition to Stratocaster guitars made early on for Eric Johnson, Eric Clapton, and David Gilmour, Stevens and Page were soon crafting Custom Shop Strats for Pete Townshend, Yngwie Malmsteen, Robert Cray, Cesar Rojas, and others. Hobbyists, weekend warriors, and serious collectors alike were also discovering that the Custom Shop was the place to acquire one-offs, special limited editions, and the best recreations of vintage Fender Stratocaster guitars available.

LEFT: *A later Custom Shop "Blackie" reproduction.* BELOW LEFT: *Eric Johnson, a long-time proponent of elevated Stratocaster tone.* BELOW RIGHT: *Yngwie Malmsteen with his Custom Shop Stratocaster.* OPPOSITE: *A meeting of the minds, Fender style (left to right): John Page, Eric Clapton, and Freddie Tavares.*

A Visit from Freddie

Some two years into the inception of the Custom Shop, Page says he realized that he, Stevens, and the growing team were "writing a new chapter in Fender's history." But Page also appreciated the privilege of having worked with Freddie Tavares in his previous post on the R&D team. The longest-serving key Fender employee to have spanned the days with Leo, CBS's ownership, and the FMIC management takeover, Tavares had retired from Fender in 1985 but was known to drop in on his old colleagues now and then.

"I guess around 1989," says Page, "my mentor, Freddie Tavares, came by to visit and told me that the [Custom Shop] reminded him of when he first started working for Leo Fender in the 1950s. That was monumental to me!"[6]

Delving further into his memories of this historic figure at Fender, Page recalls,

Freddie Tavares lived up to the true meaning of a mentor in my life. He selflessly offered guidance to me as a young greenhorn in R&D. Not only with the actual work, but in life . . . humor, healthy eating, relationships, humility, musicianship, and every other way you can think of. Every day started with a corny joke and ended with him making an entry in his journal of the day's activities. He was an incredibly kind and generous soul who helped shape who I became in later years.

I am reminded of something I've never shared before: In those days Freddie would write and perform a song for each of the R&D employees on their birthday. He would write special lyrics to the tune of "Many Happy Returns of the Day." So, when Freddie's seventieth birthday came along, I wrote and performed an original song for him. It was inspired by all the stories he told me of his life, and especially his early years spent in his beloved Hawaii. Working with this lovely man, sharing the same office designing Fender Guitars, was one of the highlights of my life."[7]

Tavares, an inductee into the Steel Guitar Hall of Fame, spent much of his retirement returning to performing, largely donating his time to entertain residents of nursing homes and senior living facilities. He died in Anaheim, California, in July 1990 at the age of seventy-seven and is buried on the island of Oahu, Hawaii.

Growth and Key Departures

By the time of its tenth anniversary, the Custom Shop had grown to include sixty employees working in its own space that had expanded to thirty-thousand square feet. In addition to the many skilled "team builders" in the department, several skilled luthiers from within Fender at large were named "master builders." Sought out by the collectors and the stars alike, early members of this elite group included George Blanda, Fred Stuart, J. W. Black, Gene Baker, Mark Kendrick, and Alan Hamel, all of whom were producing truly custom-grade instruments, crafted entirely by hand. From the 1990s into the 2000s, the master builder roster increased further, adding several others whose names are now well-known in guitar circles, including John English, John Suhr, Stephen Stern, and Chris Fleming.

Michael Stevens departed Fender in 1990, returning to Texas to set up his own one-man shop. In November 1998, John Page turned over his position as head of the Custom Shop to Mike Eldred and moved over to become executive director of the Fender Museum of Music and the Arts Foundation. He then departed Fender entirely and moved to southern Oregon in 2003, where he designed and built functional art furniture before returning to the craft of guitar-making in more recent years. His departure from the Custom Shop was partly inspired by the reorganization of its team in a different space in the new factory in Corona. The new $20 million factory brought Fender's diverse departments from several buildings together under one roof in a massive 177,000-square-foot facility. The company also made several concessions toward zero-toxic-emissions finishing and several general improvements in efficiency. The part Page played in getting Fender back on its feet and reestablishing the Stratocaster in particular remains prominent in his mind to this day:

Designing and creating in the Fender Custom Shop was the perfect realization of my dream career as a designer. To be able to create totally unique versions of the Stratocaster and other iconic Fender instruments, outside of the parameters to be mass producible, was an amazing experience. As a designer [budget considerations] can be stifling. In the Custom Shop, a lot of those restrictions were lifted.

If it was a special run, like the 90th Harley-Davidson Anniversary Stratocaster or the 40th Anniversary Playboy, it was up to us to create it with very limited restrictions. And, with one-off art pieces like the *L'Oiseau de Feu* [Bird of Fire] Stratocaster and others, all restrictions were gone—the sky was the limit. Personally, having been involved in the development of these instruments that in and of themselves were wonderful examples of musical instrument art, could have been enough for anyone. But having them be "real" Fender Stratocaster guitars, and being part of their creation, and having had a role in the Stratocaster's seventy-year legacy, begets an honor of magnitude beyond description.[8]

OPPOSITE, CLOCKWISE FROM TOP LEFT:
John Page at his desk in the mid-period Custom Shop. Gene Baker, one of a handful of master builders who translated independent success to the Custom Shop. Master builder J. W. Black at the Custom Shop woodpile. George Blanda, a master builder with the Custom Shop virtually since its inception.

Fender

ABOVE: *A completed guitar awaits testing on the Custom Shop rack.* **OPPOSITE:** *The hands of master builder Alan Hamel at work.*

Making Them Old Again

Some of the most popular Custom Shop Stratocaster guitars for nearly thirty years have been those of the Relic Series, launched in 1995. At the time, the notion of an intentionally "aged," "antiqued," or "distressed" guitar was not entirely new, and such techniques had occasionally been employed for a variety of reasons: to match the wear on existing parts of vintage guitars when other parts were restored or replaced, to produce reproduction-style guitars for performing artists who wanted them to match vintage examples in their collections, or—to more ignominious ends—to create forgeries intended to be passed off as originals to unwary buyers. The Fender Custom Shop's Relic Series, however, marked the first time a major guitar maker had applied such processes to produce highly accurate renditions of its own golden-age instruments, and the results struck a chord with countless players.

Builders at the Custom Shop occasionally dabbled in some elements of what has come to be called "factory aging" in the early 1990s, well before the Relic Series was officially launched. The oft-told tale is that this began when Keith Richards said he would play a Custom Shop guitar if they "bashed it up a bit." That, however, is apocryphal. Coincidentally, it was another artist who was working with the Rolling Stones at that time who likely requested the first pre-aged guitar from the Custom Shop.

"I saw Don Was at his studio on Mulholland Drive in LA," says former master builder J. W. Black, "when he was recording the Stones in the early '90s, and he said he was attending the Grammys. Bonnie Raitt was nominated, and he was her producer, and they were going to perform together. He had a new bass and wanted to know if we could 'beat up' or distress the instrument so it wouldn't look like new sneakers on the playground."[9]

It would seem the notion of production of a pre-aged guitar was working its way into the Custom Shop's thinking via several avenues well before a formal process to make the Relics part of the line was established. Black recalls that after his visit from Don Was, he was working on ageing the body of a black Stratocaster that would become the first Relic-finish guitar prototype. Prior to working at Fender, Black had done ageing on vintage-guitar restorations (to help restored parts match original parts), so it wasn't a new concept to him.

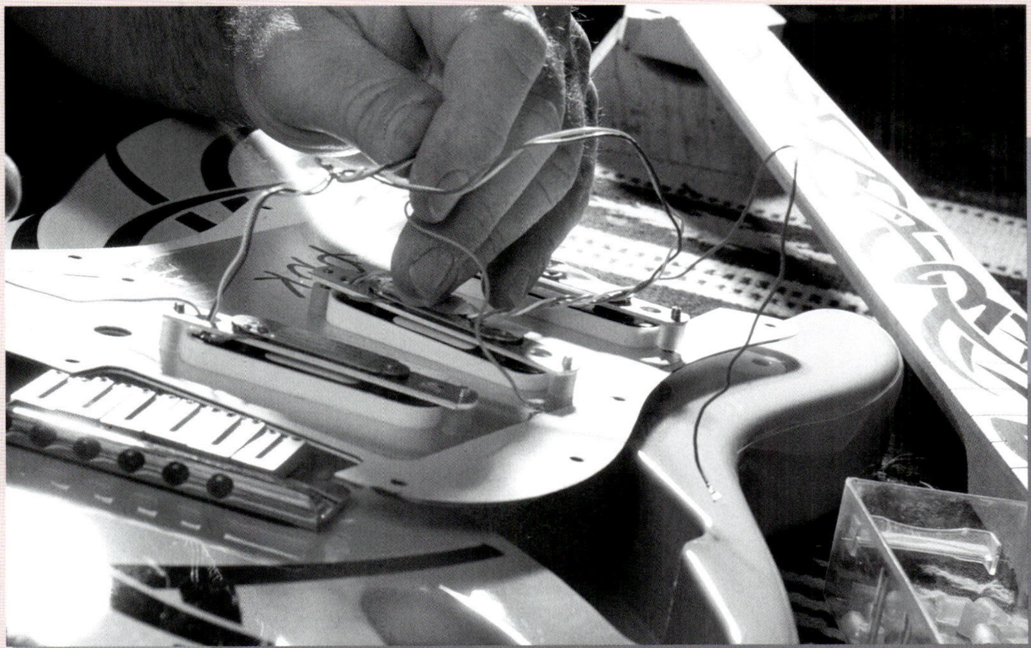

LEFT: *Vince Cunetto with bodies awaiting the Relic treatment.*
BELOW: *Custom Color bodies awaiting the Cunetto touch.*

"I thought I gave the black proto to Pierre De Beauport from the [Rolling] Stones," Black reported, "but I was later reminded that I'd given it to Kenny Wayne Shepherd. The second proto did go to Pierre, and that was a Mary Kaye with a birds-eye neck and completely done by Vince."

The seed was planted, even if it wouldn't grow substantially for a few years. And it turns out Black had already made the acquaintance of the craftsman who could help Fender bring it to fruition.

The "Vince" of Black's recollection—Vince Cunetto—describes himself as having been "one of those kids who always liked to take things apart," a tendency he applied with the passion of a fanatic to his love of vintage Fender guitars in adulthood. He was working a day job in the broadcast side of the advertising industry in Kansas City, Missouri, when he and J. W. Black were introduced in the early '90s by a joint acquaintance, Jim Colclasure, a vintage guitar dealer.

"I started trading, buying, and selling vintage guitars on the side in '84 or '85," says Cunetto. "I got hit with the bug to have a vintage Telecaster of my own, but I couldn't afford any of the ones I was trading myself, so I started farting around with trying to age guitars . . . doing a lot of research into Telecasters and blueprinting them. I'd borrow Telecasters from Jim and I'd machine pin-router templates, and I would buy the wood and I'd take it to a company that had a nice old pin-routing machine, and I started making Telecaster bodies. Then I started finishing them. When I was a kid I had worked in this body shop, and that's how I learned to spray lacquer."[10] From there, he also taught himself to make dead-accurate vintage decals, and all the pieces were in place.

As Cunetto recalls, the connection between his private builds and Fender began with the most basic of components: an aged pickguard that he showed to Black. "And J. was like, 'Wow, that's kind of cool. What if we did a whole guitar?' And I was like, 'Well, I've been doing them for a long time!'"

Black made it clear, Cunetto relates, that any independent production of complete, aged, vintage-style "Fenders" couldn't be condoned, but if he were to do such work *for* Fender, that might be a different matter. Initially, Black used Cunetto to create period-correct logo decals for one-offs and short runs, and aged parts such as a distressed Bakelite pickguard, which Black used to restore Ron Wood's vintage blackguard Telecaster. And that's how it went for a time, in bits and pieces, until the vintage-replica master and the master builder realized that they could apply this thinking to a much grander scheme. Black ran it up the flagpole to Page, his boss at the Custom Shop, and the pair decided to give it a try, commissioning a prototype from Cunetto.

"Vince sent John [Page] and I an aged '60s-style Strat in gold metallic," says Black. "All the parts and finish on the guitar were aged and patinaed to look like an authentic vintage instrument. It was very convincing and was on the cusp of being a counterfeit. We decided to use Vince to make a couple of prototypes for the [winter '95] NAMM show: a '50s Nocaster in aged butterscotch Blonde and an aged '57 Stratocaster in two-tone Sunburst."[11] That was when Page had a sneaky notion: "Don't tell anybody! Do it under the radar. Don't tell anyone in Fender management, and we'll keep it in the Custom Shop."

(CONTINUED ON PAGE 178)

THIS PAGE: *A 1996 Cunetto Mary Kaye Stratocaster, now a collector's item nearly thirty years after its creation.* **OPPOSITE:** *The first Cunetto Relic prototypes, ready for the 1995 NAMM show.*

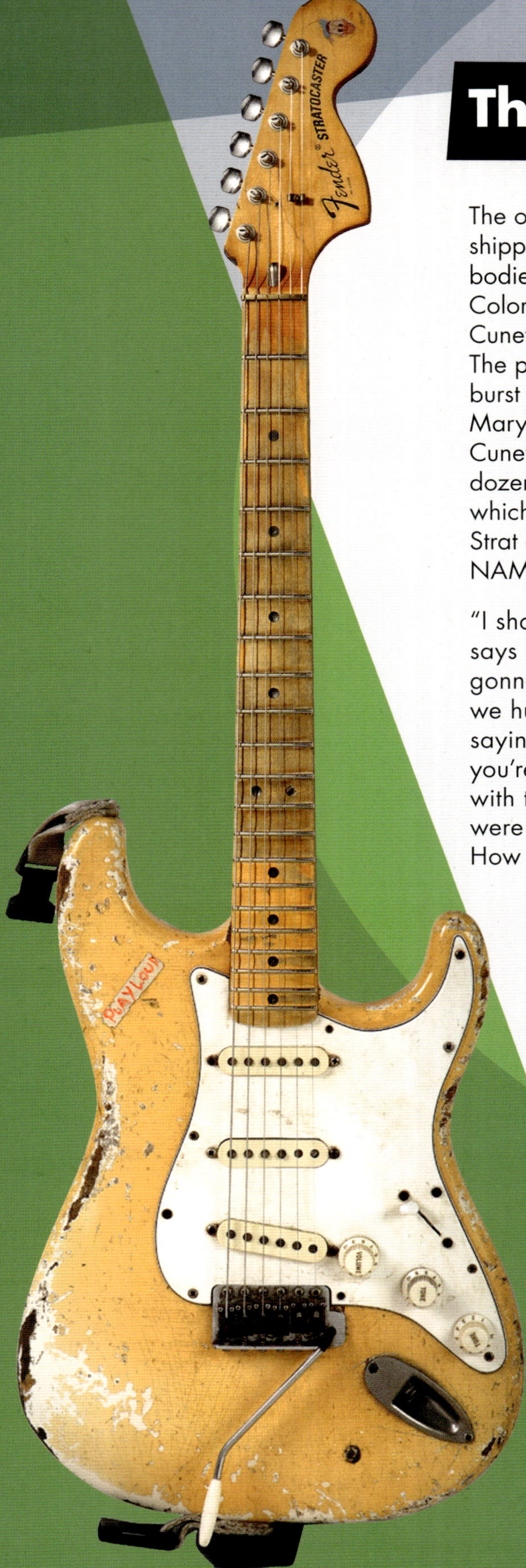

The Relics Arrive

The original process involved Black shipping boxes of Fender Custom Shop bodies, necks, and parts to Cunetto in Colorado, where he then resided, which Cunetto would finish, age, and return. The pair changed the plan from a sunburst '60s Stratocaster to a Blonde '57 Mary Kaye, and by December of 1994, Cunetto had completed around half a dozen acceptable prototypes, from which Black and Page selected one Strat and one Nocaster to display at NAMM a month later.

"I showed up at the NAMM show," says Cunetto, "because J. said 'You're gonna' want to be here for this!' And we hung them up, and people were saying, 'Wow, that's really cool that you're paying homage to your history with these old guitars!' And the reps were like, 'Yeah, they're *new* guitars. How many do you want?' And that was it. *That* was it!" Both Black and Cunetto recall that Mike Lewis, who was head of Fender's marketing department at the time, was very supportive of the venture. "He looked at [the Relic-finished guitars]," says Cunetto, "and he was like, 'Hell yeah, we're going to do this! Who wouldn't want to play this? You could take this guitar at any time on any stage and put it in somebody's hand, and they'd say, "Yeah, I'll play that!"'"[12]

Although the original intention was to have Cunetto train Custom Shop builders to produce the Relics finishes, for the first few years, they were made in a facility in Springfield, Missouri, by a team he put together there, while Fender gradually scaled up to take on the work at the Custom Shop in Corona. Now often referred to as "Cunetto Relics," the Stratocaster guitars from these early years took hold quickly, firmly establishing the notion of an officially factory-aged guitar from Fender. Shortly after Page's departure from the Custom Shop, new head Mike Eldred brought the Relic Series in-house.

LEFT: *The latest incarnation of the Custom Shop's Malmsteen Strat—apparently intended to be played loud.* OPPOSITE: *A Heavy Relic Stratocaster displays playing wear intended to represent a hard life on the road.*

ABOVE LEFT: *Master builder Todd Krause finishes up a Robbie Robertson Last Waltz Stratocaster.* **ABOVE RIGHT:** *Robertson with the original in 1987.* **OPPOSITE LEFT:** *In 2023, Todd Krause's Michael Landau "Coma" Stratocaster, based on the session ace's '59, showed just how far a "player's vintage" guitar can be pushed.* **OPPOSITE RIGHT:** *The team-built Tyler Bryant "Pinky" Stratocaster is another example of Custom Shop creations that continue to push the envelope.*

Eldred also refreshed the lineup at that time, introducing the popular Time Machine Series that presented '50s maple-board and '60s rosewood-board Stratocaster guitars in three different levels of distress: Relic, Closet Classic (gently aged), and New Old Stock (or NOS—vintage style but unaged). This three-tiered series had a long and successful run—although the Relic finishes always sold in the greatest numbers—and has further evolved in recent years. Around the late 2000s and early 2010s, some custom orders and short runs began to be aged to what was termed "Heavy Relic" and "Ultra Relic" condition, adding increasing levels of distress to the existing gradations. The Relic treatment has been applied to several Limited Editions, Dealer Select, and Anniversary models in the years since its inception.

In 2015 Eldred departed the Custom Shop, and its oversight was taken up by Mike Lewis, vice president of product development and an early proponent of the Relic Series. Further expanded at that time, the Time Machine offerings now included, ranked in levels of ageing from none to most: NOS, Closet Classic, Lush Closet Classic, Journeyman Relic, Relic, and Heavy Relic. Many players and product reviewers alike agree that the current range of Fender Relic models includes some of the finest factory-distressed guitars the Custom Shop has ever produced.

The Original Hot Rod Rolls On

In addition to the reputation it has earned for its own guitars, the Custom Shop has made an impact on Fender as a whole, operating as a testing ground for myriad procedures, innovations, and *retro*-vations that have permeated all guitar-making departments at Fender. Custom-wound pickups, hot-rodded circuitry, specially tooled hardware, custom neck shaping and fret selection, and other elements of creatively elevated builds represent the kinds of player-centric craftsmanship that makes Custom Shop guitars truly special, while also inspiring changes in other Fender guitars made both in the US and the plant in Ensenada, Baja California, Mexico.

Whether it was Abigail Ybarra re-creating the best of Fender's golden-age pickups, Josefina Campos custom-winding new and innovative pickup designs, or master machinist Scott Buehl creating an RSD Telecaster and Jaguar/Jazzmaster bridge, the Custom Shop craftspeople are continually innovating. And while all are applied first and foremost to making Custom Shop guitars into truly special instruments, some elements of the R&D process also filter down to everything from American Elite Series guitars, to Classic Series Roadworn models, to the Mod Shop interactive Fender.com portal, and beyond.

At the time of writing, the current generation of master builders includes Yuriy Shishkov, Todd Krause, Dennis Galuszka, Dale Wilson, Paul Waller, Jason Smith, Ron Thorn, Kyle McMillin, Vincent van Trigt, Austin MacNutt, Andy Hicks, and David Brown. Building upon the Custom Shop's reputation for exalted Artist and Limited Edition models, several creations from these craftsmen stand out in recent years.

The *Game of Thrones* House Targaryen Stratocaster crafted by Ron Thorn in 2020 brought new levels of artistry to a themed guitar built in collaboration with the producers of one of the most popular television series of our time. In 2023, the Michael Landau "Coma" Stratocaster by Todd Krause showed the heights to which the archetypal "player's vintage" guitar can be pushed when the beloved modified '59 Strat of one of the most acclaimed artists of his generation meets the talents of a top-flight luthier. And recent artist models including the 2021 George Harrison "Rocky" Stratocaster (Paul Waller), 2022 Limited Mike McCready 1960 Stratocaster (Vincent van Trigt), 2023 Jerry Garcia "Alligator" Stratocaster (Austin MacNutt), and 2023 Limited Edition Tyler Bryant "Pinky" Stratocaster (team built) continue to push the envelope.

Ron Thorn was the Fender Custom Shop's sole supplier of custom inlay work from the mid-'90s on, as well as a highly respected independent custom-guitar maker, before being hired by the Custom Shop in 2018 as a principal master builder and named director of the Custom Shop before his departure in 2023. From his perspective, moving from a small shop to a department within one of the world's largest and most respected guitar makers proved a surprisingly natural transition, thanks to the attitude of both his colleagues on the manufacturing floor and the management that oversees the work.

Eric Clapton tests a Custom Shop re-creation of Brownie through an EC Series Twinolux amp.

Fender

"Fender might be a huge corporation, but it's still a hot rod shop here," says Thorn. "These guys are still willing to take chances, and are digging it, and are cool about it. Everybody's a player—so they're just nerded out! It doesn't matter what job they have. They can be the sanders, the fret installers, there are some really good players here, and they're so proud to be working on Fenders, and I'm right there with them. I'm just stoked to be here and it's a great product, and everybody's thrilled by it."[13]

As acclaimed as the Custom Shop's work has been since its very inception, Thorn's oversight and an ongoing push to make this "the best of the best" continue to elevate the quality and attention to detail seen in this department's output today. Long apparent in the elite Master Built guitars, such consistency and next-level achievement now plays through in all of the Custom Shop's team-built instruments as well. (At the time of writing, these are produced in six standard series: Vintage Custom, Artisan, Limited Edition, American Custom, Postmodern, and Time Machine, which are frequently joined by Limited Edition Series and special runs for authorized Custom Shop dealers.)

Summing up the current attitude in the department, Thorn concludes, "In this day and age there's no excuse for sloppy builds. Pickup routes that don't look right or are wonky, that stuff really bothers me. So, I feel that precision and fine woodworking is a must for a high-quality instrument, especially coming from the Custom Shop. There's no way any of the builders would tolerate something like that. That, I feel, is paramount."[14]

ABOVE: *Checking Custom Shop Relic plastics against the original Brownie's pickup covers.* **OPPOSITE:** *Master builder Ron Thorn sands a Stratocaster neck.*

HARLEY DAVIDSON

TOP AND ABOVE: *Master builder Yuriy Shishkov at work in 2014 on his Fabergé Pine Cone Easter Egg Stratocaster, and the completed guitar.* **LEFT AND OPPOSITE:** *The 2023 Jerry Garcia "Alligator" Stratocaster from the bench of luthier Austin MacNutt is based on the 1955 Stratocaster that Graham Nash gifted to Garcia in 1971.*

Chapter

9

ONWARD INTO THE NEW ERA

A Strat for Every Garage

By the mid-'80s, FMIC's new owners had a solid plan going forward. Manufacturing in Japan had ably bridged the gap while the team got Fender America up and running, and it continued to feed important markets with both Fender Japan and Squier models. The range of Stratocaster guitars already available at this point established a stratum that has remained—and even expanded—to this day: whereas from 1954 to the early 1980s, there was essentially only one Stratocaster model available at any given time (albeit in a wide variety of finish options and sometimes with the option of either maple or rosewood fingerboard and hardtail or vibrato bridge), hereafter there would be a Fender-made Stratocaster to suit every budget and every stylistic requirement. From Squier to Custom Shop and from Vintage Reissue and Relic to American Standard, Plus, Elite, and Ultra, the Strat was busting out all over, in every conceivable variation. Going forward, there was a Strat for every garage, basement, stage, and studio, and they would all be made by Fender.

Bonnie Raitt was the first female artist to be honored with a Custom Shop signature guitar.

From Standard to Plus

After testing the waters just before the change of ownership with "advanced" models such as the Strat and the Elite Stratocaster, both gone by the time the buyout was complete, FMIC balanced the popular American Vintage Reissue with two new advanced models in 1986 and 1987, dubbed the American Standard and the Stratocaster Plus.

The American Standard essentially replaced the so-called Dan Smith Standard Stratocaster and was something of a descendant of the core model (if we exclude the Vintage Reissue). It consolidated the return to a smaller vintage-era headstock and four-bolt neck attachment, albeit with the internal Micro-Tilt adjustment system that eliminated the need to use shims to adjust the neck angle. Its updates included a modern two-post bridge with block saddles, enclosed tuners, and a 22-fret neck. The model became a long-running favorite, surviving a name change to American Series Stratocaster and performing simply as "a Stratocaster" to most players who used one.

The Stratocaster Plus took the American Standard platform and upgraded it further with a roller nut, locking tuners, and Lace Sensor hum-rejecting pickups. Developed by Don Lace Sr. in 1985 and used exclusively by Fender from 1987 to 1996, Lace Sensors were genuine single-coil pickups designed with internal metal "claws"—not entirely unlike those surrounding Fender's Jaguar pickups but unseen beneath the solid covers—which refocused the magnetic field and reduced sixty-cycle hum.

The draw of hum-reducing pickups led to the use of Lace Sensors on several Artist models that followed the Stratocaster Plus, some of which also shared other contemporary features. Fender's first non–Custom Shop Eric Clapton Stratocaster carried three Lace Sensor pickups along with vintage-style vibrato and tuners and a TBX mid-boost circuit. Robert Cray also had a Lace Sensor–loaded Signature Strat in the same era, and the Jeff Beck Signature Stratocaster had other Strat Plus–like features, along with *two* Lace Sensors wired side by side in the bridge position that could be used together as a pseudo-humbucker or as a single-coil, plus others individually wired in the middle and neck positions.

OPPOSITE: *Details of an American Standard Stratocaster, made in Corona, California.* THIS PAGE: *A 1989 Stratocaster Plus shows off its two-post vibrato bridge, Lace Sensor noiseless pickups, and Wilkinson roller nut.*

Strat Goes Super and a Dozen

Launched in 1988 from the Japanese factory and 1989 or 1990 from Corona, the H. M. Strat represented Fender's first serious counterattack at the so-called superstrats that other makers had been aiming at the metal and heavy rock markets for several years. Based on a slightly smaller body with less broadly radiused edges, the H. M. Strat carried a humbucking pickup in the bridge position with single-coils in the middle and neck positions, along with a Kahler locking vibrato and locking nut and a 24-fret neck built on a 25" [63.5 cm] scale length.

Japanese-built H. M. Strats had DiMarzio Super Distortion humbuckers and locally built single-coils, whereas the American models carried a DiMarzio Super 3 humbucker and two of the same single-coil pickups used by the American Standard. It seems the H. M. Strat wasn't much of a hit, however, even with the crowd that it was intended to please, and it was discontinued after 1992. It's possible that the players who could use a Stratocaster of that configuration were well used to getting it from other makers by this point, and most purists rejected the radical rejig out of hand.

Originally made in Japan from 1988 to 1996, and occasionally thereafter, the Strat XII was a twelve-string electric configured with a bridge and elongated dual-six-per-side headstock but was otherwise much like a traditional hardtail Stratocaster. It was Fender's first production twelve-string electric since the Electric XII of the '60s, and the first-ever Stratocaster twelve-string (the Electric XII shared body lines with the offset Jazzmaster and Jaguar designs).

Fender's H. M. Stratocaster was a Superstrat for the ages, with 24 frets, double-locking vibrato, and a humbucker in the bridge position.

South to Mexico

Production in Japan had proved successful for several years when the Japanese yen doubled in value in 1987, putting a serious squeeze on the profitability of the import line. The American Standard Stratocaster of 1986 had helped keep a strong mid-priced model in the market, but Fender suddenly needed a means of production to suit lower price points, and a factory in Mexico made perfect sense.

In 1987 Fender had begun employing a handful of workers in a converted church in Ensenada, Baja California, Mexico, doing nonmanufacturing work such as packing strings and accessories. It became apparent that a full-fledged factory in that location—just over the border and only 180 miles south of Fender's American home in Corona, California—would yield myriad benefits. In addition to allowing easy collaboration and quality control, lower labor costs and overheads in the Mexican location also enabled the production of several lower-priced lines to suit the North American market, while Japanese production could largely be redirected to the Japanese domestic market and other regions within and closer to Asia.

Relocated to a much larger facility on the south side of Ensenada in 1989, the Ensenada plant was first put to work revitalizing Fender's amplifier manufacturing. Guitars joined the line in 1991 after considerable help from several consultants from the FujiGen Gakki plant in Japan, where Fender guitars had been manufactured for nearly ten years.

"FujiGen brought their machinery with them, plus five or six people," former Fender CEO Bill Mendello later told author Tony Bacon. "We opened up our Mexican operation, and FujiGen trained the people, using their techniques. So, the manufacture of guitars in Mexico was more Japanese-like than it was US-like. We had a few people from the USA help them, but for the most part the training, the techniques, the painting—all were Japanese."[1]

Guitar production in Ensenada hit around 175 instruments a day by 1992 and had ramped up to 600 a day by 1995, following the rebuilding of the factory after a fire in '94. By 1998 the Ensenada facility boasted a workforce approximately 40 percent larger than that of the main facility in Corona, one that was producing nearly twice the number of instruments. By this time, Mexican-made Fender guitars had also far supplanted the guitars of Fender Japan as the company's main export line and represented a comprehensive range across several styles and price points.

Through the course of the '90s, the Ensenada factory introduced several variations on the Stratocaster template that would experience enduring popularity, most of them recognized for their appealing blend of quality and affordability. Among them were the Classic '50s, '60s, and '70s Stratocaster guitars, which delivered key features of Strats from these distinct eras. Production further expanded into several creatively revised and modified renditions of longtime favorites, including the Traditional Fat Strat, Deluxe Powerhouse Strat, and Tex-Mex Strat. The latter, with vintage-inspired aesthetics and some modern updates for improved playability, is a perennial favorite that was renamed the Jimmie Vaughan Tex-Mex Stratocaster in 1996.

BOTH: *Building the American Standard HSS Stratocaster.*

In 2011 Fender also applied a touch of the Custom Shop's Relic Series to Mexican-made guitars with the popular Road Worn Series, which brought that played-in look and feel in a much more affordable price range. Since then, Mexican-made Fender instruments and amplifiers have continued to deliver great value in several classic and creative models and continued to evolve through several popular new lines as a major part of Fender's Stratocaster stable.

TOP: *Bill Schultz (left) visits the rebuilt Mexican factory after the 1994 fire.* **ABOVE:** *Bill Schultz celebrates ten years of Ensenada production with his Mexican colleagues.* **OPPOSITE:** *Manufacturing Stratocasters in Ensenada: applying Fender decals to Classic Series '50s Strats, soldering electrical components, and large-headstock '70s Stratocaster necks awaiting assembly.*

Fender STRATOCASTER
Fender STRATOCASTER
WITH SYNCHRONIZED TREMOLO

SERIAL NUMBER MZ8216530
MADE IN MEXICO

Jimmie Vaughan puts a Tex-Mex Stratocaster through its paces at the 2008 NAMM show.

Corona Goes Big

Ever since the purchase of Fender from CBS in 1985 FMIC had been badly in need of a comprehensive facility in Corona. The corporate headquarters had been moved to Scottsdale, Arizona, in 1991 but manufacturing remained in California. By the late '90s production at that location had spread across ten buildings and a total of 115,000 square feet of space, leading to some predictable hassles for dispersed departments seeking to collaborate. With the Ensenada plant fully up to speed and able to take up the slack, in 1998 Fender built a new, state-of-the-art factory in Corona.

An obvious boon to production efficiency, the new $20 million, 177,000-square-foot building also enabled considerable upgrades to Fender's environmental and sustainability standards. For one, the new facility included a zero-toxic-emissions finishing department, which was not only key for statutory compliance with California's strict environmental codes, but also it enabled Fender to bring production of the Relic Series guitars entirely back in-house.

Meanwhile, in 1995 Fender released the first Signature model for a female artist, the Bonnie Raitt Stratocaster. Bearing the large headstock of Raitt's own long-time No. 1, a late-'60s Stratocaster, the Signature model nevertheless eschewed the original's stripped finish and brown wood stain for a range of appealing colors, including a sumptuous Blue Burst with pearloid pickguard. The model marked the continuation of a receptive market for Fender's Signature models, which would boom considerably in following years.

Back to the Future

By the mid-'90s, Fender's post-CBS design and production efforts had proven extremely successful, and the company was primed to continue its creative diversification into several sectors eager to embrace Stratocaster guitars that were differently appointed and variably priced. The American Vintage Reissue Series continued to underpin the lineup by reminding players of the company's golden age while making such guitars available at relatively reasonable prices. A bevy of new models added in 2012 represented classic Stratocaster guitars from alternative years in the '50s and '60s, while the name of the line itself was slightly modified to the American Vintage Series.

Then, although its popularity hadn't waned in the slightest, the entire vintage-inspired lineup from Fender America was thoughtfully overhauled in 2018. Now encompassed within the American Originals Series of guitars and basses, American-made Stratocaster guitars took on the specs and cosmetics of Strats from the '50s, '60s, and '70s and spanned a wider range of original models than either preceding series. Almost in the blink of an eye, however, midway through 2022, Fender phased out the American Originals in favor of an impressive new American Vintage II Series.

(CONTINUED ON PAGE 202)

RIGHT AND NEXT SPREAD: *An American Vintage Reissue 1965 Stratocaster. The lineup reminded players of the company's golden age—at reasonable prices.*

WIRING DIAGRAM
3-POSITION SW
STRATOCASTER®
Fender® AMERICAN VINTAGE SERIES
MODERN WIRING
RIGHT HAND
Fender AMERICAN Vintage SERIES
Your new American Vintage instrument is designed to be an accurate reproduction of an iconic Fender instrument from the past. This includes a thin, nitrocellulose lacquer finish that has the feel and characteristics of those great old vintage instruments Fender is renowned for.
Possible "checking" or cracking and texture of the wood grain on this thin lacquer finish are the normal result of duplicating the original Fender finishes.
Please read the Fender Lacquer Finishes: Precautions and Care booklet included in your Accessory Kit for more information on the care and feeding of your American Vintage instrument.
www.fender.com/americanvintage
Fender® fine electric instruments
Parts Kit
p/n 9543700
FINE EL
Fender
stratocaster
INSTRU
MANU
distributed exclusively by
Fender
SANTA ANA, CALIFORNIA
Fender INSTRUCTION MANUAL FOR STRATOCASTER

LEFT HAND
TRUMENTS
Fender

Where many previous vintage-inspired, non–Custom Shop Stratocaster guitars had either missed a period-correct detail or two, or had very consciously "benefited" from some modernized specs in the name of playability, such as 9.5" [24.1 cm] fingerboard radii, the American Vintage II guitars were the result of Fender's deep dive into specs and documentation from the years in which the target guitars were made, thereby representing as holistic a vintage redux as current-day tooling, components, and budgets would allow.

"The iconic models in the American Vintage II Series are a near 1:1 comparison with their original predecessors," said Justin Norvell, executive vice president of product. "Today they are built with precise, modern manufacturing processes that weren't available in the past."[2]

Amid a raft of Telecasters, Jazzmasters, and basses, the American Vintage II Series included Stratocaster guitars pinned to 1957, 1961, and 1973. Each boasted neck profiles representative of their intended origins—a full soft V on the '57, rounded medium C on the '61, and a fatter '70s C on the '73—along with period-correct specs such as 7.25" [18.4 cm] fingerboard radii and pickups wound and constructed according to the particulars of their respective years. The '57 and '61 boasted genuine nitrocellulose finishes in three characteristic colors, while the '73 carried a polyurethane finish (generally considered preferable to the thick polyester that was sprayed at the time) in the characteristic Mocha and Aged Natural of the '70s, as well as Lake Placid Blue.

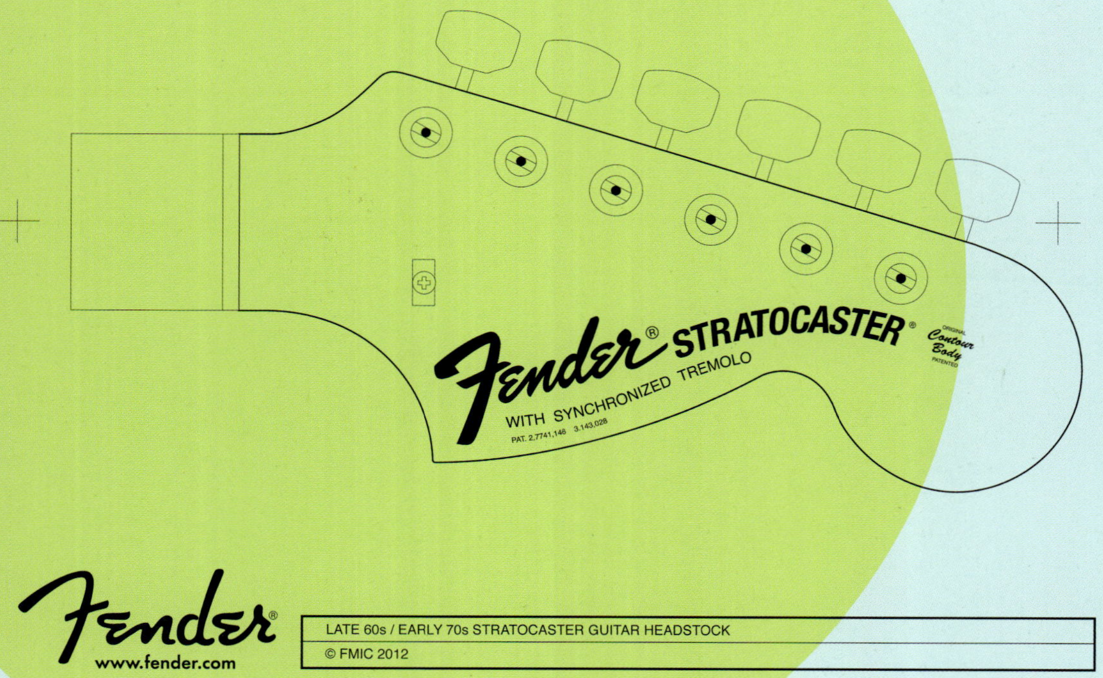

THIS PAGE: *The design rendering for a reissue '69 Stratocaster headstock, and the creation itself.* OPPOSITE: *The JV Modified Stratocaster celebrates early Japanese Fender production.*

Updates in Offshore Vintage

Coasting in under the wire just ahead of the American Vintage II, the Stratocaster guitars of Fender's JV Modified were unveiled in early summer of 2022 and represented the first time in more than two decades that a standard-issue model for the US market was manufactured in Japan. The "JV" in the name stood for "Japanese Vintage," but players familiar with the early Japanese Fenders will recognize it as the prefix to a coveted early run of Stratocaster guitars manufactured at the FujiGen Gakki factory. The "Modified" reveals that they aren't strict reissues. As such, the range simultaneously pays homage to these great guitars while adding features that help increase the versatility of these well-made but relatively affordable Strats.

The JV Modified '50s Stratocaster came in two-tone Sunburst with the maple neck characteristic of the era, plus uncharacteristic medium-jumbo frets and a humbucker in the bridge position that could be split for single-coil tones via a push-pull switch on the lower tone control. The JV Modified '60s Stratocaster aimed a little later in the decade than most '60s reissues of the past, with the large headstock of the post-'65 guitars but a four-screw neck attachment for its maple neck. Mods included medium-jumbo frets and a push-pull switch on the lower tone control to add the neck pickup to pickup positions 1 and 2, as desired.

The more affordable Fenders from the Ensenada plant in Mexico had already seen a revamp in 2019 with the introduction of the Vintera Series. Living up to its premise of capturing "**Vint**age style for the modern **era**"—as the compound name declared—this line delivered a striking number of new and interesting models in a wide range of options. All in all, the Vintera Series included a whopping nineteen variations of eight different guitars and basses (not including various finish and neck-shape options). Four Stratocaster guitars graced the series, offering '50s and '60s renditions in both standard and Modified variations.

As might be expected, the guitars lacking the "Modified" tag were offered with a raft of vintage-inspired features, including period-appropriate woods and neck profiles, narrow vintage frets, 7.25" [18.4 cm] fingerboard radii, and pickups revoiced to more accurately represent their mid-'50s and early '60s inspirations. The Modified renditions include two-post vibratos, flatter 9.5" [24.1 cm] fingerboard radii, medium-jumbo frets, Hot-'50s and Hot-'60s single-coil pickups, and an S-1 switch (positioned within the center of the volume control's knob) that adds the neck pickup to selector positions 1 and 2 when engaged.

The Shawbucker and Moods for Moderns

In a fascinating case of "déjà vu all over again," in the mid-2010s, the quest for a more toneful humbucking pickup was fulfilled by another engineer who had moved from Gibson to Fender. Much as the co-creator of the legendary PAF humbucking pickup, Seth Lover, had done in the late '60s before developing Fender's Wide Range Humbucking Pickups, former Gibson engineer Tim Shaw took a position as chief engineer at Fender and proceeded to revitalize the maker's position in high-quality humbuckers.

In the earlier part of his career, Shaw was known for developing a Gibson humbucker that took the design closer to its hallowed late-'50s roots after many years of declining quality, resulting in highly praised units in upper-level guitars produced from around 1980 to 1985. Shaw's work for Fender revitalized the engine room of several models loaded with Shawbucker humbuckers, such as the one prominently displayed in the bridge position of the HSS-configured 2015 Fender American Standard Stratocaster Shawbucker. Shaw has since applied his skills to several variations of more traditional Fender single-coil pickups, while Shawbuckers are used in a range of humbucker-equipped models.

THIS PAGE: *The American Standard evolves: the American Professional II Stratocaster.*
OPPOSITE: *A 2015 American Standard Stratocaster HSS. Tim Shaw's work for Fender revitalized several models by loading them with Shawbucker humbuckers.*

After relaunching its flagship line of contemporary Stratocaster guitars in the American Standard Series as the American Professional Series in 2017, Fender thoroughly revamped these offerings just three years later as the American Professional II Series. Perhaps most notable in the Strats of this series was Fender's clever leaning on vintage-inspired aesthetics, while more seamlessly blending the best of '50s, '60s, and ultra-modern features into an impressively high-performance package.

Available in two renditions—with three single-coils (SSS) or with a humbucker in the bridge position (HSS)—the American Professional II Stratocaster guitars included their own very comfortable deep-C neck profiles with rolled fingerboard edges, modern two-post vibratos that nevertheless carried bent-steel saddles and cold-rolled steel inertia blocks, sculpted neck heels with offset four-screw attachment and Micro-Tilt adjustment, V-Mod pickups wound specifically to enhance each of their three positions, treble-bleed circuits, and other clever details.

But that's not all, folks! Radiating in both directions, pricewise, from this thoughtful reboot, Fender's full American-made Stratocaster range encompassed another three series—not including the American Vintage II Series or Custom Shop guitars already discussed: the American Performer, American Ultra, and American Luxe lines.

At list prices of around fifteen percent less than the American Professional II models, the American Performer guitars all presented a blend of vintage components and modern specs. The two Stratocaster guitars in the range comprised a model with three single-coil pickups and a large late-'60s-into-'70s headstock (with truss-rod adjustment accessed at the headstock end), along with nifty updates like twenty-two medium-jumbo frets, a 9.5" [24.1 cm] fingerboard radius, and Fender's Greasebucket tone circuitry. First seen on the Highway One Series of 2005, the Greasebucket circuit reduces highs without adding bass as the tone control is turned down. The HSS rendition had similar appointments with a humbucker in the bridge and push-pull switching for coil splitting.

Toward the latter part of 2019, Fender introduced the American Ultra Stratocaster in SSS and HSS configurations and followed up in 2021 with the American Ultra Luxe Stratocaster. Both carry the smaller headstock and have similar contemporary details such as a tapered neck heel, "Ultra" rolled fingerboard edges, noiseless pickups, an S-1 switch in the volume knob to add the neck pickup, and locking tuners. Some of the upgrades on the Ultra Luxe were subtle—a painted headstock and an "Augmented D" neck shape versus "Modern D" on standard Ultra—but the top model also marked the first time a production Stratocaster had been made with stainless-steel frets. The Luxe was also available with a Floyd Rose double-locking vibrato system and a humbucking pickup in the bridge position.

The American Ultra Stratocaster, with humbucker, two-post vibrato, and pushbutton switching within the Volume control.

Stars' Guitars

We have already visited the Artist Signature Stratocaster guitars made in the mid-1980s for Eric Clapton, a Fender first that has been followed by a long and successful line of Signature models. The Yngwie Malmsteen model followed hot on its heels—featuring the Swedish virtuoso's preferred scalloped fretboard and a two-post vibrato—along with the Jeff Beck Stratocaster, complete with modified features and a parallel set of Lace Sensor single-coil pickups wired side-by-side in the bridge position—after which a veritable dam burst of artist-inspired models ensued from both Corona and Ensenada.

Fender has had a long list of productive collaborations with name artists over the years, a trend in Artist Signature models that largely began with the Custom Shop but spread throughout the lines over the past couple of decades. Through the Stratocaster's seventieth anniversary and undoubtedly beyond, a plethora of Artist Signature models have remained among Fender's most popular, and most interesting, offerings.

At the time of writing, the entire Artist Signature Series from both Corona and Ensenada numbers more than fifty guitars strong (excluding the Custom Shop offerings), and Stratocaster guitars accounted for a sizeable proportion of those—approximately half!

In 2020 Fender brought a clever twist to the Artist Signature concept with its ambitious new Stories Collection, launched with the Eric Johnson "Virginia" Stratocaster. Designed to capture the vintage look of Johnson's former prized original 1954 Stratocaster—a rare early Strat made with sassafras wood rather than ash—plus a few artist-introduced modifications, the guitar was produced in a Limited Edition by the Custom Shop, followed with one year of production at the Corona factory. "When I got the prototype from Fender," Johnson commented, "it had the tone I had been looking for since my original guitar. It has a particularly smooth, sustained tone, but as you turn it up it has gain like a little violin."[3]

R&B star H.E.R. debuted her own Signature Artist model at the 2019 Grammy Awards in the form of a clear acrylic Stratocaster made by Custom Shop Master Builder Scott Buehl, which was followed with an Ensenada-made Limited Edition with alder body in exclusive Blue Marlin or Chrome Glow finishes. From the Tom Morello Stratocaster with Floyd Rose and kill switch, to the Jimi Hendrix Stratocaster with reversed bridge pickup and headstock, to the Jim Root Stratocaster with hardtail bridge and active EMG humbucking pickups, to the Stevie Ray Vaughan Stratocaster with reversed (left-handed) vibrato unit, to the Dave Murray Stratocaster with Seymour Duncan Hot Rails and Mini JB pickups and double-locking Floyd Rose vibrato, several Signature Artist models have proved fertile ground for special appointments and even extreme modifications.

Others—such as the Signature Artist Strats for Cory Wong, Robert Cray, Buddy Guy, Lincoln Brewster, Jimmie Vaughan and more—lean further toward traditional looks and specs, but always with plenty of artist-specific twists to make them special.

Eric Johnson in the studio with his Thinline Signature Stratocaster.

One particularly notable latter-day Signature Artist model from the Stories Collection is the Michael Landau Coma Stratocaster, first re-created in meticulous detail as a limited-edition Custom Shop rendition by master builder Todd Krause, followed by a more accessible take from the Corona factory. Following the "precise" and "homage" routes, respectively, these creations pay tribute to the world-renowned session ace's beloved 1959 Stratocaster—affectionately nicknamed "Coma"—which morphed from a Floyd Rose–equipped superstrat with built-in boost circuit to a semi-restored state with six-screw vibrato, Wide Range Humbucker in the bridge position, and two Ultra Noiseless single-coil Strat pickups in the middle and neck positions.

For four decades Signature Artist Stratocaster guitars have celebrated the many ways in which notable stars have made this legendary guitar their own, and the series will undoubtedly remain a big part of Fender's formula for success going forward.

BELOW: *The H.E.R. Stratocaster in Chrome Glow finish. The R&B star debuted her clear acrylic Signature Artist model at the 2019 Grammy Awards.* BOTTOM: *Tom Morello of Rage Against the Machine and Audioslave holds aloft his "Soul Power" Artist model Stratocaster based on the modified Designer Series Stratocaster used during his time in Audioslave.* OPPOSITE: *The Jimi Hendrix Artist Tribute Stratocaster, fully reversed for the right-handed player seeking the left-handed experience.*

experience
Photo: Tony Gale / Star File, Inc.
Clothing courtesy of the Bob Terry Collection
The Jimi Hendrix Stratocaster®
Fender
©1996 FMIC

Chapter

10

SOARING INTO THE FUTURE

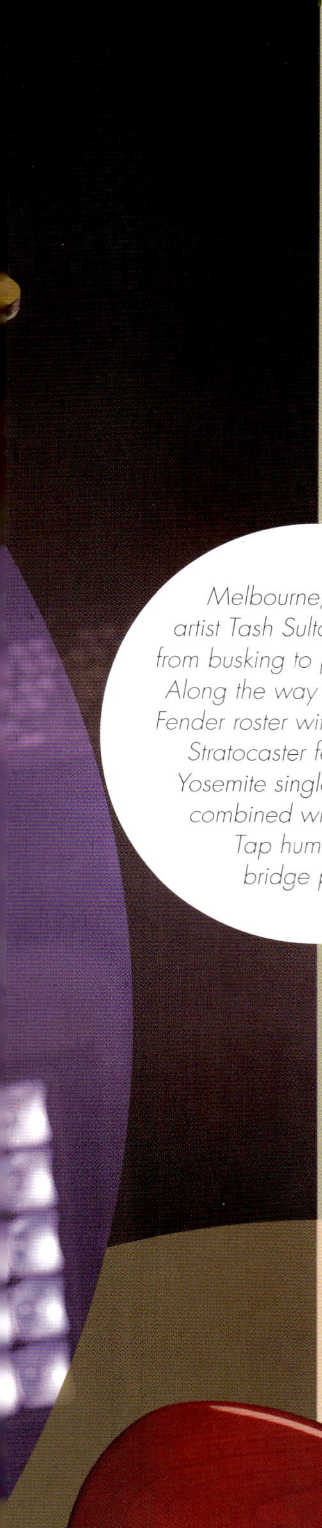

Melbourne, Australia, artist Tash Sultana has gone from busking to playing arenas. Along the way she joined the Fender roster with this Signature Stratocaster featuring two Yosemite single-coil pickups combined with a Double Tap humbucking bridge pickup.

Form Follows Function

The Fender Stratocaster is often spoken of as the most influential, and most imitated, electric guitar ever created, and there's no sign of that changing as the design rolls through its seventieth anniversary and deep into the twenty-first century. And working hand in hand with all the "Leo got it right the first time" magic that has kept a circa-1954 design relevant is Fender Musical Instrument Corporation's unwavering intention to look toward the future while continuing to appreciate what it accomplished in the past.

FMIC CEO Andy Mooney has made it clear that the Stratocaster's place in a future music world won't be found in some high-tech, digitally equipped eStrat or iFender but in coupling the model's traditional strengths and capabilities with new interfaces for learning, recording, and performing.

"Guitar players have rejected technology embedded within guitars for years," says Mooney, "as the technologies employed didn't solve a problem and were often poorly executed. Leo Fender's designs are timeless because his design philosophy was that form must follow function. . . . Leo believed that artists were angels, and his job was to give them wings to fly. This has become Fender's vision statement, and continues to guide everything we do. Today, we're equally focused on serving the needs of first-time players with products and services like Fender Play. . . . We not only strive to give future artists the wings to fly, we strive to teach them *how* to fly."[1]

Hybrid Tones and a California Redux

One arguably futuristic reconfiguration of the seminal design that has proven impressively popular since its unveiling in 2020 is the Acoustasonic Stratocaster, which followed on the heels of the Acoustasonic Telecaster released the year before. Including models built in both the California and Ensenada factories, the Acoustasonic Stratocaster is a genuine hybrid acoustic-electric that employs a slimline hollow body rendered on the Strat's iconic lines, with a traditional bolt-on neck. Put it all together and it's a package that feels familiar to electric players yet extends the sonic boundaries into a wealth of realistic acoustic tones.

The guitar combines a Fender- and Fishman-designed Acoustic Engine fed by a piezo under-saddle pickup and Fender's patented Stringed Instrument Resonance System (SIRS) embedded within the guitar's top to not only produce strikingly realistic acoustic tones but also alter them to replicate a range of styles and tonewood combinations. The acoustic signal can be blended with the more traditional electromagnetic Fender Acoustasonic Noiseless pickup, or either system can be tapped and amplified individually.

Organizationally, the opening of a new FMIC headquarters in Los Angeles in 2017 after many years in Scottsdale, Arizona, returned Fender much closer to its original stomping grounds of Fullerton, some thirty miles to the southeast. With famed recording studios Sunset Sound and United Recording virtually on the new headquarters' doorstep, as well as easy access to the hub of the music industry that LA has so long represented, the move made practical sense too.

"We specifically picked out this location because of the proximity to everything," said Mooney. "Not only because of the nearby studios or visits from artists, but also because of our ability to attract fresh talent to the digital organization."[2]

ABOVE: *The Alternate Reality Sixty-Six presents a playful twist on a retro-modern direction in which the Stratocaster might have gone.* **OPPOSITE:** *The Acoustasonic Stratocaster represents a bold new hybrid of acoustic and electric tone and playability.*

Fender

Education and Evolving Demographics

One side of the new tech that will continue to move Fender forward into the future, and the Stratocaster along with it, involves music education in the digital arena. Mooney has already mentioned Fender Play's roll in forming a conduit between new players and the maker, and he also foresees FMIC's future growth tied to the young- and novice-player markets in other big ways. Noting the trends, Fender isn't fretting over the supposed "post-rock" era or worrying that kids are less driven to emulate their guitar heroes than they were, say, three, four, or five decades ago. Instead, FMIC is embracing the trends toward guitar as a leisure item as much as a form of virtuosity.

"I saw the shift beginning in guitar with the advent of punk," says Mooney. "Punk, I think, opened up an aperture to playing the instrument. It was less about the virtuosity and more about having fun and self-expression. I think that applies both to bands and individuals who just wanted to pick up the instrument and master it to their own comfort level and enjoy playing songs in small groups or on their own."[3]

In addition to this subtle shift in motivation, research conducted by Fender in 2018 indicated that half of new amateur guitarists in the US and UK are women, and women have also been notable for their predominance among more successful new bands. A quick survey of women playing guitar in indie-rock, punk, blues, and rock bands shows that Fender has been dominant lately as guitar of choice for several of these artists. Certainly, Fender offsets like the Jaguar, Jazzmaster, and Mustang have been having a moment lately, and several notable players—beabadoobee, Alvvays frontwoman Molly Rankin, Courtney Barnett, and Snail Mail's Lindsey Jordan among them—are prominently wielding guitars from these series. Even so, leading artists in a broad range of genres have continued to confirm the Stratocaster's unbridled versatility and power, including Canadian country singer Lindsay Ell, blues supremo Ana Popovic, Rebecca Lovell of Larkin Poe, Ritzy Bryan of The Joy Formidable, and plenty of others.

As much uncertainty as there might be in the world, the one certain thing for the Stratocaster's future is that its appeal, playability, and versatility will keep it relevant for as long as music is made.

THIS PAGE: *A wave of creative artists continues to take the Stratocaster legend forward, including (clockwise from top left) Lindsay Ell, Ana Popovic, Rebecca Lovell of Larkin Poe, and Ritzy Bryan of The Joy Formidable.* OPPOSITE: *Fender Play epitomizes the company's outreach to learning players.*

References

CHAPTER ONE

1. Richard Smith, *Fender: The Sound Heard 'Round the World* (Hal Leonard, 2003), 7.
2. Leo Fender, interview by *Guitar Player Magazine*, September 1971.
3. Ibid.
4. Leo Fender, interview by *Guitar Player Magazine*, May 1978.
5. Tony Bacon, "George Fullerton, Leo Fender's Longtime Partner, on Their Legacy of Guitar Building," Reverb.com, February 8, 2018.
6. Detlef Schmidt, *Fender Precision Basses: 1951–1954* (Centerstream Publishing, 2010), 109.
7. Leo Fender, interview by *Guitar Player Magazine*, February 1984.

CHAPTER TWO

1. Tony Bacon and Barry Moorhouse, *The Bass Book* (GPI Books, 1995), 9.
2. Shannon Wianecki, *Hanahou*, September 2012.
3. A. R. Duchossoir, *The Fender Stratocaster* (Hal Leonard, 1994), 7.
4. John Page, interview by the author, March 2023.
5. Mark Knopfler, interview by BBC, November 2008.
6. Tony Bacon, "An Oral History of the Fender Stratocaster," Reverb.com, June 11, 2019.
7. Tom Wheeler, *The Stratocaster Chronicles* (Hal Leonard, 2004), 44.
8. Tom Wheeler, *The Stratocaster Chronicles* (Hal Leonard, 2004), 50.
9. Tony Bacon, "An Oral History of the Fender Stratocaster," Reverb.com, June 11, 2019.
10. Tony Bacon, "Fender's Don Randall Offers Revisionist Take on Leo, CBS, and the Company's Early Days," Reverb.com, November 1, 2018.
11. Richard Smith, *Fender: The Sound Heard 'Round the World* (Hal Leonard, 2003), 127.
12. Tony Bacon, "George Fullerton, Leo Fender's Longtime Partner, on Their Legacy of Guitar Building," Reverb.com, February 8, 2018.

CHAPTER THREE

1. Chris Fleming, interview by the author, November 2005.
2. Forrest White, *Fender: The Inside Story* (Miller Freeman Books, 1994), 44.

CHAPTER FOUR

1. A. R. Duchossoir, *The Fender Stratocaster* (Hal Leonard, 1994), 17.
2. Robert Perine, *Vintage Guitar*, May 2003.

CHAPTER FIVE

1. Chris Fleming, interview by the author, November 2005.

CHAPTER SIX

1. Forrest White, *Fender: The Inside Story* (Miller Freeman Books, 1994), 146.
2. Leo Fender, interview by *Guitar P layer Magazine*, September 1971.
3. Robert Perine, *Vintage Guitar*, May 2003.
4. Tony Bacon, "Fender's Don Randall Offers Revisionist Take on Leo, CBS, and the Company's Early Days/ Bacon's Archive," Reverb.com, November 1, 2018.
5. Don Randall, NAMM Oral History Interviews, 2006.

CHAPTER SEVEN

1. Tony Bacon and Paul Day, *The Fender Book* (Balafon Books, 1998), 58.
2. Bill Schultz, NAMM Oral History Interviews, March 2003.
3. John Page, interview by the author, October 2019.
4. John Page, interview by the author, March 2023.
5. Bill Schultz, NAMM Oral History Interviews, March 2003.
6. Leslie Berkman, *Los Angeles Times*, February 2, 1985.

CHAPTER EIGHT

1. Michael Stevens, interview by the author, September 2017.
2. John Page, interview by the author, September 2017.
3. Michael Stevens, interview by the author, September 2017.
4. John Page, interview by the author, September 2017.
5. Michael Stevens, interview by the author, September 2017.
6. John Page, interview by the author, September 2017.
7. John Page, interview by the author, March 2023.
8. Ibid.

9. J. Black, interview by the author, September 2017.
10. Vince Cunetto, interview by the author, September 2017.
11. J. Black, interview by the author, September 2017.
12. Vince Cunetto, interview by the author, September 2017.
13. Ron Thorn, interview by the author, March 2019.
14. Ibid.

CHAPTER NINE

1. Tony Bacon, "35 Years of Fender Mexico: A Timeline," *Guitar World*, July 2022.
2. Justin Norvell, Fender American Vintage II press release, October 2022.
3. Eric Johnson, Fender.com, February 2020.

CHAPTER TEN

1. Andy Mooney, interview by the author, July 2020.
2. Rob LeDonne, "Guitar Maker Fender Steps into the Future While Remaining Steeped in Its Past," *Billboard*, May 4, 2018.
3. Amy X. Wang, "Fender Is Expanding Its Audience through More Than Just Guitars," *Rolling Stone*, October 18, 2018.

Image Credits

a = above; b = bottom; c = center; i = inset; L = left; m = main; r = right; t = top

All photos Fender Musical Instruments Corporation, except:

Alamy Stock Photos: 61tr, *Sydney Morning Herald*; 61br, Pictorial Press; 78t, KEYSTONE Pictures USA; 115, ZUMA Press; 157, Gijsbert Haanskroot; 158, John Alashian; 168bL, John Alashian; 212, Stian S. Moller; 217tL, Media Punch; 217tr, CTK; 217br, Lasse Lagoni; 217bL, Yui Mok. **Courtesy of Dirk Bakker, Artbook:** 71b. **Bridgeman Images:** 70r. **Creative Commons:** 13bL and 13br, BarbieS76; CCA-SA 3.0 Unported. **Photos by Joe Dampt:** 150 –151. **Courtesy of Davidson's Well-Strung Guitars:** 54L, 54r, 55L, 55r, 59mr, 59br, 66, 67r, 70tL, 71 all, 79t, 80–81, 82c, 83t, 83b, 84, 85, 88–89, 90–91, 96, 100, 106t, 106b, 108–109 all, 110–111 all, 114, 125bL, 125r, 128, 130 all, 134. **Michael Dregni:** 43b. **Courtesy of Rick Falkiner Guitar Centre, Sydney:** 102L, 102r, 125t. **Getty Images:** 26, Michael Ochs Archives; 61tL, Roger Viollet; 61bL, Carl Iwasaki/The Chronicle Collection; 68, Michael Ochs Archives; 75tL, David Redfern; 75tr. GAB Archive/Redferns; 76m, Michael Ochs Archives; 77c, Michael Ochs Archives; 117, Michael Ochs Archives; 118, Michael Ochs Archives; 120, David Redfern; 129t, Ian Dickson/Redferns; 129b, Koh Hasebe/Shinko Music/Hulton Archive; 136L, Michael Putland/Hulton Archive; 136r, David Warner Ellis/Redferns; 142, Ron Pownall/Corbis Historical; 144, Leni Sinclair/Michael Ochs Archives; 180r, George Rose/Hulton Archive; 186, Gijsbert Haanskroot/Redferns; 188, Robert Knight Archive/Redferns. **Photos by David Hall:** 192–193. ***Guitarist Magazine* photo by Joby Sessions/Future Publishing Ltd:** 36. **Photos by Randy Lutz, guitar courtesy of Infinity Guitars:** 191t, 191b. **Albert Molinaro/EliteGuitars.net:** 15, 28t, 28b. **Nigel Osbourne/Jawbone Press:** 78bc, 98–99 all, 155. **Courtesy of Maddie Patch:** 13t. **John Peden:** 8. **Courtesy of Jarrod Perkins:** 63, 64–65. **Quarto Publishing Group Collection:** 12t, 69L, 70t, 75bL, 76b, 77b, 78c, 87br, 133b all, 143, 156, 159i, 161r all, 189. **Photo by Brad Rickard, guitar courtesy of Nationwide Guitars:** 153tL, 153b, 176–177 all. **Courtesy of Rumble Seat Music:** 77t, 119, 124. **Photo by John Shults, guitar courtesy of True Vintage Guitar:** 38, 40bL, 40br, 41, 43t, 44, 45t, 45b, 50, 52, 53, 59tL, 59tr, 59bL, 67b, 82t, 82b. **Courtesy of John Snyder:** 137L, 137r, 138.

Author Bio

Dave Hunter is an author, musician, and journalist. He is the author of several popular books about guitars, amps, and effects, including Motorbooks' *Fender 75 Years*. A regular contributor to *Guitar Player* and *Vintage Guitar* magazines, he resides in Kittery, Maine.

Acknowledgments

Thanks are due to a wealth of people who helped to bring this book to fruition. At Quarto, group publisher Zack Miller, project manager Brooke Pelletier, group managing editor John Gettings, group creative director Regina Grenier, designer Cindy Laun, copy editor Caitlin Fultz, and executive editor Dennis Pernu all played an enormous part in making this work what it is. At Fender, Christina Stejskal, Rich Siegle, Najla Quarry, Charnita Belcher, Richard Bussey, Sarah Park, Jessica Hoyt Protheroe, and Justin Norvell were enormously helpful in providing contacts, information, and archival images, and John Page, Michael Stevens, Chris Fleming, Vince Cunetto, Ron Thorn, and Andy Mooney offered their direct insights and observations of Fender past and present.

Thanks to David and Paige Davidson at Well Strung Guitars for photographic access to their stock of vintage Stratocasters and all the hard work in sorting and sending, and to John Shults at True Vintage Guitar for his excellent photos of several early Stratocasters. Thanks also to Jarrod Forge, Jon Snyder, Barry Witte and Dirk Witte Music, Bruce Sandler, Craig Brody and The Guitar Broker, Vince Cunetto, John Page, David Hall, Joe Dampt, Eliot Michael at Rumble Seat Music, Nigel Osbourne, John Peden, Albert Molinaro, and Randy Lutz for their generous photography submissions.

I also owe a debt of gratitude to authors Tony Bacon, Tom Wheeler, Richard Smith, and Andre R. Duchossior for laying so much invaluable groundwork in this field in the form of original interviews with personnel from the early days of Fender who are no longer with us. Thanks, as always, to my wife Jess and our children, Fred and Flo. And finally, many thanks to the readers who remain as fascinated as I do with this strange convergence of wood, wire, craftsmanship, industry, and art.

Index

Quarto.com

First Published in 2024 by Motorbooks, an imprint of The Quarto Group,
100 Cummings Center, Suite 265-D, Beverly, MA 01915, USA.
T (978) 282-9590 F (978) 283-2742

Motorbooks titles are also available at discount for retail, wholesale, promotional, and bulk purchase. For details, contact the Special Sales Manager by email at specialsales@quarto.com or by mail at The Quarto Group, Attn: Special Sales Manager, 100 Cummings Center, Suite 265-D, Beverly, MA 01915, USA.

28 27 26 25 24 1 2 3 4 5

ISBN: 978-0-7603-8516-6

Digital edition published in 2024
eISBN: 978-0-7603-8517-3

Library of Congress Cataloging-in-Publication Data

Names: Hunter, Dave, 1962- author.
Title: Fender Stratocaster 70 years / Dave Hunter.
Description: Beverly, CA : Motorbooks, 2024. | Includes bibliographical references and index. | Summary: "Gorgeously illustrated and authoritatively written, Fender Stratocaster® 70 Years is the officially licensed celebration of the legendary brand's revolutionary electric guitar"—Provided by publisher.
Identifiers: LCCN 2023041195 |
ISBN 9780760385166 | ISBN 9780760385173 (ebook)
Subjects: LCSH: Stratocaster—History. | Stratocaster—Construction.
Classification: LCC ML1015.G9 H8607 2024 | DDC 787.87/19—dc23/eng/20230901
LC record available at https://lccn.loc.gov/2023041195

Cover Photo: Jarrod Perkins
Cover Design: Cindy Samargia Laun
Page Design: Traffic
Page Layout: Cindy Samargia Laun

Printed in China